45 Vegan Recipes for Home

By: Kelly Johnson

Table of Contents

- Plant-Based Protein Power
- Vegan Chickpea Curry Delight
- Zesty Quinoa Salad Bowl
- Creamy Vegan Mushroom Risotto
- Sweet Potato and Black Bean Enchiladas
- Mediterranean Stuffed Peppers
- Vegan Lentil Shepherd's Pie
- Avocado and Tomato Bruschetta
- Spicy Thai Coconut Noodles
- Vegan Pesto Pasta
- Roasted Vegetable Buddha Bowl
- Jackfruit Tacos with Lime Slaw
- Vegan Pad Thai
- Spinach and Artichoke Stuffed Portobello Mushrooms
- BBQ Chickpea Stuffed Sweet Potatoes
- Vegan Lentil Sloppy Joes
- Creamy Cashew Alfredo with Roasted Cherry Tomatoes
- Vegan Pumpkin and Sage Risotto
- Cilantro Lime Quinoa Salad
- Teriyaki Tofu Stir-Fry
- Vegan Eggplant Parmesan
- Coconut Curry Chickpea Stew
- Vegan Broccoli and Cheese Stuffed Baked Potatoes
- Spaghetti Aglio e Olio with Roasted Vegetables
- Moroccan Chickpea and Vegetable Tagine
- Vegan Sushi Rolls
- Vegan Buffalo Cauliflower Bites
- Ratatouille with Herbed Polenta
- Creamy Vegan Tomato Basil Soup
- Chickpea and Spinach Coconut Curry
- Vegan Stuffed Bell Peppers
- Mexican Street Corn Salad
- Vegan Black Bean Burgers
- Lemon Garlic Roasted Brussels Sprouts
- Vegan Chocolate Avocado Mousse

- Vegan Caesar Salad with Crispy Chickpea Croutons
- Vegan Thai Green Curry
- Sweet and Spicy Glazed Tempeh
- Vegan Spinach and Artichoke Dip
- Vegan Blueberry Oat Muffins
- Mediterranean Chickpea Salad
- Vegan Chocolate Banana Bread
- Creamy Vegan Mac and Cheese
- Roasted Red Pepper and Walnut Pesto Pasta
- Vegan Mango Coconut Chia Pudding

Plant-Based Protein Power

Ingredients:

For the Base:

- 1 cup quinoa, cooked
- 2 cups kale, finely chopped
- 1 cup cherry tomatoes, halved
- 1 cup cucumber, diced
- 1 cup red bell pepper, diced
- 1/2 cup red onion, finely chopped
- 1/4 cup fresh parsley, chopped

For the Plant-Based Protein:

- 1 can (15 oz) chickpeas, drained and rinsed
- 1 tablespoon olive oil
- 1 teaspoon smoked paprika
- 1/2 teaspoon cumin
- Salt and black pepper to taste

For the Dressing:

- 3 tablespoons tahini
- 2 tablespoons lemon juice
- 1 tablespoon maple syrup
- 1 clove garlic, minced
- 2 tablespoons water (adjust for desired consistency)
- Salt and black pepper to taste

Optional Toppings:

- Avocado slices
- Pumpkin seeds
- Microgreens

Instructions:

Prepare the Base:

Cook Quinoa:
- Cook quinoa according to package instructions. Allow it to cool.

Chop Vegetables:
- Finely chop kale, halve cherry tomatoes, dice cucumber and red bell pepper, finely chop red onion, and chop fresh parsley.

Assemble the Base:
- In a large bowl, combine cooked quinoa, chopped kale, cherry tomatoes, cucumber, red bell pepper, red onion, and fresh parsley. Toss well.

Prepare the Plant-Based Protein:

Roast Chickpeas:
- Preheat the oven to 400°F (200°C).
- In a bowl, toss chickpeas with olive oil, smoked paprika, cumin, salt, and black pepper.
- Spread the chickpeas on a baking sheet and roast for 20-25 minutes or until crispy, shaking the pan occasionally.

Prepare the Dressing:

Make Tahini Dressing:
- In a small bowl, whisk together tahini, lemon juice, maple syrup, minced garlic, water, salt, and black pepper. Adjust the water quantity for your desired dressing consistency.

Assemble the Power Bowl:

Assemble Individual Bowls:
- Divide the quinoa and vegetable mixture into individual serving bowls.
- Top each bowl with roasted chickpeas.

Drizzle with Dressing:
- Drizzle the tahini dressing over each power bowl.

Add Toppings:
- Garnish with avocado slices, pumpkin seeds, and microgreens if desired.

Serve:
- Serve immediately and enjoy your plant-based protein power bowl!

Tips:

- Customize the power bowl with your favorite vegetables, such as roasted sweet potatoes, shredded carrots, or steamed broccoli.
- Add a squeeze of fresh lemon juice or a sprinkle of nutritional yeast for extra flavor.

This Plant-Based Protein Power Bowl is a nutrient-packed and delicious meal that combines the goodness of quinoa, vibrant vegetables, and roasted chickpeas, all topped with a creamy tahini dressing. It's not only a feast for the eyes but also a powerhouse of plant-based protein, fiber, and essential nutrients. Feel free to customize the bowl with your favorite ingredients and enjoy a wholesome and satisfying meal.

Vegan Chickpea Curry Delight

Ingredients:

For the Chickpea Curry:

- 2 cans (15 oz each) chickpeas, drained and rinsed
- 1 tablespoon coconut oil
- 1 large onion, finely chopped
- 3 cloves garlic, minced
- 1 tablespoon fresh ginger, grated
- 1 tablespoon curry powder
- 1 teaspoon ground cumin
- 1 teaspoon ground coriander
- 1 teaspoon turmeric
- 1/2 teaspoon cayenne pepper (adjust to taste)
- 1 can (14 oz) diced tomatoes
- 1 can (14 oz) coconut milk
- Salt and black pepper to taste
- Fresh cilantro for garnish

For the Quinoa:

- 1 cup quinoa
- 2 cups water
- 1/2 teaspoon salt

For Serving:

- Steamed spinach or kale (optional)
- Lime wedges

Instructions:

Prepare the Quinoa:

    Rinse Quinoa:
- Rinse the quinoa under cold water.

    Cook Quinoa:

- In a saucepan, combine the rinsed quinoa, water, and salt. Bring to a boil, then reduce the heat to low, cover, and simmer for 15-20 minutes or until the quinoa is cooked and water is absorbed. Fluff with a fork.

Prepare the Chickpea Curry:

Sauté Aromatics:
- In a large skillet or pot, heat coconut oil over medium heat. Add chopped onions and sauté until they become translucent.

Add Garlic and Ginger:
- Add minced garlic and grated ginger to the onions. Sauté for another minute until fragrant.

Spice it Up:
- Add curry powder, ground cumin, ground coriander, turmeric, and cayenne pepper. Stir well to coat the onions, garlic, and ginger with the spices.

Add Chickpeas:
- Add drained and rinsed chickpeas to the spice mixture. Stir to combine.

Tomatoes and Coconut Milk:
- Pour in the diced tomatoes and coconut milk. Stir well and bring the mixture to a simmer.

Simmer:
- Let the curry simmer for 15-20 minutes to allow the flavors to meld. Season with salt and black pepper to taste.

Garnish and Serve:
- Garnish the chickpea curry with fresh cilantro. Serve over the cooked quinoa.

For Serving:

Optional Greens:
- Serve the chickpea curry over a bed of steamed spinach or kale if desired.

Lime Wedges:
- Serve with lime wedges on the side for an extra burst of freshness.

Enjoy:
- Enjoy your Vegan Chickpea Curry Delight!

Tips:

- Customize the level of spiciness by adjusting the amount of cayenne pepper.

- Feel free to add your favorite vegetables like spinach, kale, or bell peppers to the curry for added nutrition and color.

This Vegan Chickpea Curry Delight is a hearty and flavorful dish that brings together the wholesome goodness of chickpeas, aromatic spices, and creamy coconut milk. Served over a bed of fluffy quinoa, this curry is not only satisfying but also packed with plant-based protein and essential nutrients. The addition of fresh cilantro and lime wedges adds a delightful touch, enhancing the overall taste of the dish. Enjoy a delightful culinary journey with this vegan curry that is sure to become a favorite in your plant-based repertoire!

Zesty Quinoa Salad Bowl

Ingredients:

For the Quinoa Salad:

- 1 cup quinoa, rinsed
- 2 cups water
- 1/2 teaspoon salt
- 1 can (15 oz) black beans, drained and rinsed
- 1 cup corn kernels (fresh, frozen, or canned)
- 1 cup cherry tomatoes, halved
- 1 red bell pepper, diced
- 1/2 red onion, finely chopped
- 1 avocado, diced
- Fresh cilantro for garnish

For the Zesty Lime Vinaigrette:

- 1/4 cup olive oil
- 2 tablespoons lime juice
- 1 teaspoon Dijon mustard
- 1 clove garlic, minced
- 1 teaspoon honey or maple syrup
- Salt and black pepper to taste

Optional Additions:

- Sliced jalapeños for extra heat
- Crumbled feta or Cotija cheese for a tangy touch

Instructions:

Cook the Quinoa:

    Rinse Quinoa:
- Rinse the quinoa under cold water.

Cook Quinoa:
- In a saucepan, combine the rinsed quinoa, water, and salt. Bring to a boil, then reduce the heat to low, cover, and simmer for 15-20 minutes or until the quinoa is cooked and water is absorbed. Fluff with a fork and let it cool.

Prepare the Zesty Lime Vinaigrette:

Whisk Dressing:
- In a small bowl, whisk together olive oil, lime juice, Dijon mustard, minced garlic, honey or maple syrup, salt, and black pepper. Adjust the seasoning to taste.

Assemble the Quinoa Salad Bowl:

Combine Ingredients:
- In a large bowl, combine cooked quinoa, black beans, corn, cherry tomatoes, red bell pepper, red onion, and diced avocado.

Drizzle with Dressing:
- Drizzle the zesty lime vinaigrette over the quinoa salad. Toss gently to coat the ingredients evenly.

Garnish:
- Garnish the salad with fresh cilantro.

Optional Additions:
- Add sliced jalapeños for extra heat or crumbled feta or Cotija cheese for a tangy touch.

Serve:
- Serve the Zesty Quinoa Salad Bowl immediately or refrigerate until ready to serve.

Enjoy your Zesty Quinoa Salad Bowl!

Tips:

- Feel free to customize the salad with your favorite vegetables or herbs.
- For added protein, you can include grilled chicken, shrimp, or tofu.

This Zesty Quinoa Salad Bowl is a refreshing and nutritious dish that combines the goodness of quinoa with a medley of vibrant vegetables and a zesty lime vinaigrette. It's a versatile recipe that can be enjoyed as a light lunch, dinner, or a side dish for gatherings. The combination of black beans, corn, tomatoes, and avocado adds a delightful mix of flavors and textures. The zesty lime vinaigrette ties everything together with a burst of citrusy goodness. Whether you enjoy it as a standalone meal or a side, this quinoa salad bowl is a delicious and wholesome choice.

Creamy Vegan Mushroom Risotto

Ingredients:

- 1 1/2 cups Arborio rice
- 1 cup sliced cremini mushrooms
- 1 cup sliced shiitake mushrooms
- 1 small onion, finely chopped
- 3 cloves garlic, minced
- 4 cups vegetable broth, heated
- 1 cup dry white wine
- 1/2 cup nutritional yeast
- 1/4 cup vegan butter
- 2 tablespoons olive oil
- Salt and black pepper to taste
- Fresh parsley, chopped, for garnish

Instructions:

Sauté Mushrooms:
- In a large pan, heat olive oil over medium heat. Add sliced cremini and shiitake mushrooms. Sauté until they release their moisture and become golden brown. Remove a portion of the mushrooms for garnish and set aside.

Sauté Onions and Garlic:
- In the same pan, add chopped onions and minced garlic. Sauté until the onions are translucent.

Add Arborio Rice:
- Add Arborio rice to the pan and cook for 2-3 minutes, stirring frequently until the rice is lightly toasted.

Deglaze with Wine:
- Pour in the dry white wine and stir until most of the liquid has been absorbed by the rice.

Add Broth Gradually:
- Begin adding the heated vegetable broth one ladle at a time. Allow the liquid to be absorbed before adding the next ladle. Stir frequently.

Continue Cooking:
- Continue adding broth and stirring until the rice is creamy and cooked al dente. This process may take about 18-20 minutes.

Stir in Vegan Butter and Nutritional Yeast:
- Once the rice is cooked, stir in vegan butter and nutritional yeast. This will add creaminess and a cheesy flavor to the risotto.

Season and Garnish:
- Season with salt and black pepper to taste. Stir in the sautéed mushrooms that were set aside earlier. Garnish with fresh chopped parsley.

Serve Immediately:
- Serve the creamy vegan mushroom risotto immediately while it's hot.

Tips:

- Use a good-quality dry white wine for added flavor.
- Feel free to add other vegetables like spinach, peas, or asparagus for extra color and nutrition.
- Stirring frequently is key to achieving a creamy consistency.

This Creamy Vegan Mushroom Risotto is a decadent and satisfying dish that captures the rich and creamy essence of traditional risotto without using dairy. The combination of cremini and shiitake mushrooms adds depth of flavor, while nutritional yeast contributes a cheesy taste. With each spoonful, you'll experience the velvety texture and delightful umami notes of this comforting risotto. Serve it as a main dish or a side for a special occasion or a cozy night in. Enjoy the luxurious and cruelty-free indulgence of a classic mushroom risotto!

Sweet Potato and Black Bean Enchiladas

Ingredients:

For the Filling:

- 2 medium sweet potatoes, peeled and diced
- 1 can (15 oz) black beans, drained and rinsed
- 1 red bell pepper, diced
- 1 small red onion, finely chopped
- 2 cloves garlic, minced
- 1 teaspoon ground cumin
- 1 teaspoon chili powder
- 1/2 teaspoon smoked paprika
- Salt and black pepper to taste
- 2 tablespoons olive oil

For the Enchilada Sauce:

- 2 cups tomato sauce
- 1 teaspoon ground cumin
- 1 teaspoon chili powder
- 1/2 teaspoon garlic powder
- Salt and black pepper to taste

For Assembly:

- 8-10 small flour or corn tortillas
- 2 cups vegan shredded cheese
- Fresh cilantro, chopped, for garnish
- Sliced avocado, for serving

Instructions:

Prepare the Filling:

Roast Sweet Potatoes:

- Preheat the oven to 400°F (200°C). Toss the diced sweet potatoes with 1 tablespoon of olive oil, cumin, chili powder, smoked paprika, salt, and black pepper. Spread them on a baking sheet and roast for 20-25 minutes or until tender.

Sauté Vegetables:
- In a pan, heat the remaining 1 tablespoon of olive oil. Sauté red bell pepper, red onion, and minced garlic until softened. Add the black beans and roasted sweet potatoes. Mix well and cook for an additional 2-3 minutes. Set aside.

Prepare the Enchilada Sauce:

Make Enchilada Sauce:
- In a saucepan, combine tomato sauce, ground cumin, chili powder, garlic powder, salt, and black pepper. Simmer over low heat for 5-7 minutes, stirring occasionally. Adjust the seasoning as needed.

Assembly:

Preheat Oven:
- Preheat the oven to 375°F (190°C).

Assemble Enchiladas:
- Spoon a portion of the sweet potato and black bean filling onto each tortilla. Roll them up and place them seam side down in a baking dish.

Pour Sauce and Add Cheese:
- Pour the enchilada sauce over the rolled tortillas. Sprinkle vegan shredded cheese over the top.

Bake:
- Bake in the preheated oven for 20-25 minutes or until the cheese is melted and bubbly.

Garnish and Serve:
- Garnish with chopped cilantro and serve with sliced avocado.

Enjoy your Sweet Potato and Black Bean Enchiladas!

Tips:

- If using corn tortillas and find them difficult to roll without cracking, you can soften them by briefly heating each tortilla on a dry skillet for a few seconds on each side.
- Customize the filling by adding ingredients like spinach, corn, or diced jalapeños.
- Adjust the level of spice by adding more or less chili powder and smoked paprika according to your taste preferences.

These Sweet Potato and Black Bean Enchiladas offer a delightful combination of sweet and savory flavors wrapped in a warm tortilla. The roasted sweet potatoes, black beans, and vibrant spices create a filling that's both hearty and satisfying. Topped with a homemade enchilada sauce and vegan cheese, this dish is a crowd-pleaser that can be enjoyed for dinner or special gatherings. The garnish of fresh cilantro and sliced avocado adds a burst of freshness to complement the rich flavors of the enchiladas. Enjoy this plant-based twist on a classic Mexican favorite!

Mediterranean Stuffed Peppers

Ingredients:

For the Stuffed Peppers:

- 4 large bell peppers, halved and seeds removed
- 1 cup quinoa, cooked according to package instructions

For the Filling:

- 1 can (15 oz) chickpeas, drained and rinsed
- 1 cup cherry tomatoes, halved
- 1/2 cup Kalamata olives, chopped
- 1/2 cup cucumber, diced
- 1/4 cup red onion, finely chopped
- 1/4 cup fresh parsley, chopped
- 1/4 cup fresh mint, chopped

For the Dressing:

- 3 tablespoons olive oil
- 2 tablespoons red wine vinegar
- 1 teaspoon Dijon mustard
- 1 clove garlic, minced
- Salt and black pepper to taste

For Topping:

- Crumbled feta cheese (optional)

Instructions:

Preheat Oven:
- Preheat the oven to 375°F (190°C).

Prepare Peppers:

- Cut the bell peppers in half and remove the seeds and membranes. Place them in a baking dish.

Cook Quinoa:
- Cook quinoa according to package instructions.

Prepare Filling:
- In a large bowl, combine cooked quinoa, chickpeas, cherry tomatoes, Kalamata olives, cucumber, red onion, parsley, and mint.

Make Dressing:
- In a small bowl, whisk together olive oil, red wine vinegar, Dijon mustard, minced garlic, salt, and black pepper.

Combine Filling and Dressing:
- Pour the dressing over the quinoa mixture and toss until everything is well coated.

Fill Peppers:
- Spoon the quinoa filling into each bell pepper half, pressing down gently to pack the filling.

Bake:
- Cover the baking dish with aluminum foil and bake in the preheated oven for 25-30 minutes or until the peppers are tender.

Optional Topping:
- If desired, sprinkle crumbled feta cheese over the stuffed peppers during the last 5 minutes of baking.

Serve:
- Remove from the oven and serve the Mediterranean Stuffed Peppers warm.

Garnish:
- Garnish with additional fresh herbs and a drizzle of olive oil, if desired.

Enjoy your Mediterranean Stuffed Peppers!

Tips:

- Feel free to customize the filling with additional ingredients such as artichoke hearts, roasted red peppers, or pine nuts.
- Adjust the seasoning and acidity of the dressing to suit your taste preferences.
- These stuffed peppers can be served as a main dish or a flavorful side dish.

Vegan Lentil Shepherd's Pie

Ingredients:

For the Lentil Filling:

- 1 cup dry green or brown lentils, rinsed and drained
- 3 cups vegetable broth
- 1 tablespoon olive oil
- 1 large onion, diced
- 3 cloves garlic, minced
- 2 carrots, diced
- 2 celery stalks, diced
- 1 cup frozen peas
- 1 teaspoon thyme
- 1 teaspoon rosemary
- Salt and black pepper to taste
- 2 tablespoons tomato paste
- 2 tablespoons all-purpose flour
- 1 cup vegetable broth (additional, for the gravy)

For the Mashed Potato Topping:

- 4 large potatoes, peeled and diced
- 1/2 cup unsweetened almond milk (or any plant-based milk)
- 2 tablespoons vegan butter
- Salt and black pepper to taste

Instructions:

Prepare Lentil Filling:

Cook Lentils:
- In a saucepan, combine the lentils and 3 cups of vegetable broth. Bring to a boil, then reduce heat and simmer for about 25-30 minutes or until lentils are tender. Drain any excess liquid.

Sauté Vegetables:
- In a large skillet, heat olive oil over medium heat. Add diced onion, garlic, carrots, and celery. Sauté until vegetables are softened.

Add Peas and Herbs:

- Stir in frozen peas, thyme, rosemary, salt, and black pepper. Cook for an additional 2-3 minutes.

Make Gravy:
- Add tomato paste and flour to the vegetable mixture, stirring well. Gradually add 1 cup of vegetable broth, stirring continuously, until the mixture thickens to a gravy-like consistency.

Combine Lentils:
- Add the cooked lentils to the vegetable mixture, stirring to combine. Adjust seasoning if necessary.

Prepare Mashed Potato Topping:

Boil Potatoes:
- Boil the diced potatoes in a large pot of salted water until tender.

Mash Potatoes:
- Drain the potatoes and mash them with almond milk, vegan butter, salt, and black pepper until smooth and creamy.

Assemble and Bake:

Preheat Oven:
- Preheat the oven to 400°F (200°C).

Layer Lentil Filling:
- Transfer the lentil and vegetable mixture to a baking dish, spreading it evenly.

Top with Mashed Potatoes:
- Spoon the mashed potatoes on top of the lentil filling, spreading them to cover the entire surface.

Create Texture:
- Use a fork to create a textured pattern on the mashed potato topping.

Bake:
- Bake in the preheated oven for 20-25 minutes or until the top is golden brown.

Serve:
- Allow it to cool slightly before serving. Enjoy your Vegan Lentil Shepherd's Pie!

Tips:

- Customize the vegetable filling with your favorite veggies such as corn, green beans, or mushrooms.
- Feel free to add a layer of vegan cheese on top of the lentil filling before adding the mashed potatoes for an extra layer of flavor.
- Make sure to taste and adjust the seasoning of both the lentil filling and mashed potatoes according to your preference.

Avocado and Tomato Bruschetta

Ingredients:

- 1 baguette, sliced
- 2 ripe avocados, peeled, pitted, and diced
- 1 cup cherry tomatoes, halved
- 2 cloves garlic, minced
- 1/4 cup red onion, finely chopped
- 2 tablespoons fresh basil, chopped
- 1 tablespoon balsamic vinegar
- 2 tablespoons extra-virgin olive oil
- Salt and black pepper to taste

Instructions:

Preheat Oven:
- Preheat the oven to 375°F (190°C).

Toast Baguette Slices:
- Place the baguette slices on a baking sheet and toast them in the preheated oven until they are golden brown and crisp. This usually takes about 8-10 minutes. Keep an eye on them to prevent burning.

Prepare Avocado and Tomato Mixture:
- In a bowl, combine diced avocados, cherry tomatoes, minced garlic, red onion, and chopped basil.

Make Dressing:
- In a small bowl, whisk together balsamic vinegar, extra-virgin olive oil, salt, and black pepper.

Combine Ingredients:
- Pour the dressing over the avocado and tomato mixture. Gently toss until all the ingredients are well coated.

Assemble Bruschetta:
- Once the baguette slices are toasted, spoon the avocado and tomato mixture onto each slice.

Serve:
- Arrange the bruschettas on a serving platter and serve immediately.

Optional Garnish:

- Garnish with additional chopped basil or a drizzle of balsamic glaze if desired.

Enjoy your Avocado and Tomato Bruschetta!

Tips:

- To prevent the baguette slices from becoming soggy, assemble the bruschettas just before serving.
- Experiment with different varieties of tomatoes for added color and flavor.
- You can add a sprinkle of feta cheese or a pinch of red pepper flakes for additional texture and heat.

Spicy Thai Coconut Noodles

Ingredients:

- 8 oz rice noodles
- 1 can (13.5 oz) coconut milk
- 2 tablespoons red curry paste
- 2 tablespoons soy sauce
- 1 tablespoon brown sugar
- 1 tablespoon lime juice
- 2 tablespoons vegetable oil
- 1 red bell pepper, thinly sliced
- 1 carrot, julienned
- 1 zucchini, julienned
- 1 cup broccoli florets
- 1 cup snap peas, trimmed
- 3 cloves garlic, minced
- 1 tablespoon ginger, grated
- Fresh cilantro and lime wedges for garnish
- Crushed peanuts for topping (optional)
- Red pepper flakes for added heat (optional)

Instructions:

Cook Rice Noodles:
- Cook the rice noodles according to package instructions. Drain and set aside.

Prepare the Sauce:
- In a bowl, whisk together coconut milk, red curry paste, soy sauce, brown sugar, and lime juice. Set aside.

Sauté Vegetables:
- In a large pan or wok, heat vegetable oil over medium-high heat. Add sliced bell pepper, julienned carrot, julienned zucchini, broccoli florets, and snap peas. Stir-fry for 3-4 minutes until the vegetables are tender-crisp.

Add Aromatics:
- Add minced garlic and grated ginger to the vegetables. Sauté for an additional 1-2 minutes until fragrant.

Combine Sauce and Noodles:

- Pour the prepared coconut curry sauce over the sautéed vegetables. Add the cooked rice noodles. Toss everything together until well coated and heated through.

Serve:
- Divide the spicy Thai coconut noodles among serving plates. Garnish with fresh cilantro and lime wedges.

Optional Toppings:
- Top with crushed peanuts for added crunch and red pepper flakes for extra heat, if desired.

Enjoy your Spicy Thai Coconut Noodles!

Tips:

- Adjust the level of spiciness by adding more or less red curry paste according to your preference.
- Feel free to customize the vegetable selection based on your favorite choices or what's in season.
- You can add protein such as tofu, shrimp, or chicken for a heartier meal. Cook the protein separately and add it to the noodles during the final toss.
- Lime wedges and cilantro are essential for brightening up the flavors, so don't skip them!

Vegan Pesto Pasta

Ingredients:

- 8 oz (225g) of your favorite pasta (such as spaghetti or penne)
- 2 cups fresh basil leaves, packed
- 1/2 cup pine nuts
- 3 cloves garlic, peeled
- 1/2 cup nutritional yeast
- 1/2 cup extra-virgin olive oil
- Salt and black pepper to taste
- Juice of 1 lemon

Instructions:

Cook Pasta:
- Cook the pasta according to the package instructions. Drain and set aside.

Prepare Pesto:
- In a food processor, combine basil, pine nuts, garlic, nutritional yeast, and a pinch of salt. Pulse until the ingredients are finely chopped.

Add Olive Oil:
- With the food processor running, gradually add the olive oil in a steady stream. Continue processing until the mixture forms a smooth paste.

Adjust Seasoning:
- Taste the pesto and adjust the seasoning, adding more salt or nutritional yeast if desired.

Combine Pasta and Pesto:
- In a large mixing bowl, toss the cooked pasta with the prepared pesto until evenly coated.

Add Lemon Juice:
- Squeeze the juice of one lemon over the pasta and toss again to incorporate.

Serve:
- Serve the vegan pesto pasta in bowls or on plates. You can drizzle a bit more olive oil on top if desired.

Optional Garnish:
- Garnish with additional pine nuts, nutritional yeast, or fresh basil leaves.

Enjoy your Vegan Pesto Pasta!

Tips:

- Feel free to add sautéed cherry tomatoes, roasted vegetables, or your favorite vegan protein for added texture and flavor.
- Adjust the consistency of the pesto by adding more olive oil if you prefer a smoother or thinner sauce.
- Store any leftover pesto in an airtight container in the refrigerator for future use. It can also be used as a spread, sauce for pizza, or a topping for grilled vegetables.

Roasted Vegetable Buddha Bowl

Ingredients:

For Roasted Vegetables:

- 1 sweet potato, peeled and cubed
- 1 cup cauliflower florets
- 1 cup broccoli florets
- 1 red bell pepper, sliced
- 1 zucchini, sliced
- 2 tablespoons olive oil
- 1 teaspoon smoked paprika
- 1 teaspoon cumin
- Salt and black pepper to taste

For Quinoa:

- 1 cup quinoa, rinsed
- 2 cups water or vegetable broth
- Salt to taste

For Lemon Tahini Dressing:

- 1/4 cup tahini
- 2 tablespoons lemon juice
- 2 tablespoons water
- 1 tablespoon olive oil
- 1 clove garlic, minced
- Salt and black pepper to taste

Optional Toppings:

- Avocado slices
- Cherry tomatoes, halved
- Fresh cilantro or parsley, chopped
- Sesame seeds

Instructions:

Roast Vegetables:

Preheat Oven:
- Preheat the oven to 425°F (220°C).

Prepare Vegetables:
- In a large bowl, toss sweet potato, cauliflower, broccoli, red bell pepper, and zucchini with olive oil, smoked paprika, cumin, salt, and black pepper.

Roast:
- Spread the vegetables on a baking sheet in a single layer. Roast in the preheated oven for 25-30 minutes or until the vegetables are tender and golden brown, stirring halfway through.

Prepare Quinoa:

Rinse Quinoa:
- Rinse quinoa under cold water until the water runs clear.

Cook Quinoa:
- In a medium saucepan, combine quinoa and water or vegetable broth. Bring to a boil, then reduce heat to low, cover, and simmer for 15-20 minutes or until the quinoa is cooked and the liquid is absorbed. Fluff with a fork.

Prepare Lemon Tahini Dressing:

Whisk Dressing:
- In a small bowl, whisk together tahini, lemon juice, water, olive oil, minced garlic, salt, and black pepper until smooth.

Assemble Buddha Bowl:

Serve:
- Divide the cooked quinoa among serving bowls. Top with the roasted vegetables.

Add Toppings:
- Add avocado slices, cherry tomatoes, fresh cilantro or parsley, and sesame seeds.

Drizzle Dressing:
- Drizzle the lemon tahini dressing over the Buddha bowls.

Enjoy your Roasted Vegetable Buddha Bowl!

Tips:

- Feel free to customize the vegetables based on your preferences or what's in season.
- Experiment with different grains like brown rice, couscous, or farro as an alternative to quinoa.
- Adjust the thickness of the tahini dressing by adding more or less water according to your preference.

Jackfruit Tacos with Lime Slaw

Ingredients:

For Jackfruit Filling:

- 2 cans (20 oz each) young green jackfruit in water or brine, drained and rinsed
- 1 tablespoon olive oil
- 1 small onion, finely chopped
- 3 cloves garlic, minced
- 1 teaspoon ground cumin
- 1 teaspoon smoked paprika
- 1/2 teaspoon chili powder
- Salt and black pepper to taste
- 1 cup vegetable broth
- 1/4 cup tomato paste
- 2 tablespoons soy sauce or tamari
- 1 tablespoon maple syrup or agave nectar

For Lime Slaw:

- 2 cups shredded cabbage (green or purple)
- 1 carrot, grated
- 1/4 cup chopped fresh cilantro
- Juice of 2 limes
- 2 tablespoons vegan mayonnaise
- Salt and black pepper to taste

For Tacos:

- 8 small corn or flour tortillas
- Optional toppings: avocado slices, chopped tomatoes, hot sauce, chopped red onion, extra cilantro

Instructions:

Prepare Jackfruit Filling:

Sauté Onion and Garlic:
- In a large skillet, heat olive oil over medium heat. Add finely chopped onion and sauté until translucent.

Add Jackfruit and Spices:
- Add drained and rinsed jackfruit to the skillet. Use a fork to break apart the jackfruit pieces. Add minced garlic, ground cumin, smoked paprika, chili powder, salt, and black pepper. Sauté for 2-3 minutes.

Make Sauce:
- In a bowl, whisk together vegetable broth, tomato paste, soy sauce, and maple syrup. Pour the sauce over the jackfruit mixture.

Simmer:
- Reduce heat to low, cover, and simmer for 20-25 minutes, stirring occasionally. The jackfruit should absorb the flavors and have a pulled texture.

Prepare Lime Slaw:

Combine Ingredients:
- In a bowl, combine shredded cabbage, grated carrot, chopped cilantro, lime juice, vegan mayonnaise, salt, and black pepper. Toss until well combined.

Assemble Tacos:

Warm Tortillas:
- Heat the tortillas in a dry skillet or microwave until warm.

Assemble Tacos:
- Spoon the jackfruit filling onto each tortilla. Top with lime slaw and your choice of optional toppings.

Serve:
- Serve the jackfruit tacos with lime slaw immediately.

Enjoy your Jackfruit Tacos with Lime Slaw!

Tips:

- If using jackfruit in brine, make sure to rinse it thoroughly to remove any briny taste.

- Adjust the seasoning and spice level of the jackfruit filling according to your taste preferences.
- You can customize the lime slaw with additional ingredients like red cabbage, radishes, or jalapeños.

Vegan Pad Thai

Ingredients:

For Pad Thai Sauce:

- 1/4 cup tamari or soy sauce
- 2 tablespoons maple syrup or agave nectar
- 1 tablespoon rice vinegar
- 1 tablespoon lime juice
- 1 teaspoon tamarind paste (optional)
- 1 teaspoon sriracha or chili garlic sauce (adjust to taste)

For Pad Thai:

- 8 oz (225g) rice noodles
- 2 tablespoons vegetable oil
- 1 block (14 oz) firm tofu, pressed and cubed
- 1 cup broccoli florets
- 1 carrot, julienned
- 1 bell pepper, thinly sliced
- 2 cloves garlic, minced
- 2 green onions, sliced
- 1 cup bean sprouts
- Crushed peanuts for garnish
- Lime wedges for serving
- Fresh cilantro for garnish

Instructions:

Prepare Pad Thai Sauce:

> Mix Ingredients:
> - In a bowl, whisk together tamari, maple syrup, rice vinegar, lime juice, tamarind paste (if using), and sriracha. Set aside.

Prepare Pad Thai:

> Cook Rice Noodles:
> - Cook rice noodles according to package instructions. Drain and set aside.

Sauté Tofu:
- In a large skillet or wok, heat vegetable oil over medium-high heat. Add cubed tofu and cook until golden brown on all sides. Remove tofu from the skillet and set aside.

Sauté Vegetables:
- In the same skillet, add a bit more oil if needed. Sauté broccoli, julienned carrot, sliced bell pepper, and minced garlic until the vegetables are tender-crisp.

Combine:
- Add cooked rice noodles, cooked tofu, and the prepared Pad Thai sauce to the skillet. Toss everything together until well combined and heated through.

Add Green Onions and Bean Sprouts:
- Add sliced green onions and bean sprouts to the skillet. Toss for an additional 1-2 minutes.

Serve:
- Divide the Vegan Pad Thai among serving plates. Garnish with crushed peanuts, lime wedges, and fresh cilantro.

Enjoy your Vegan Pad Thai!

Tips:

- Adjust the spice level by adding more or less sriracha or chili garlic sauce to the Pad Thai sauce.
- Feel free to customize the vegetables based on your preferences.
- If tamarind paste is not available, you can use additional lime juice for a tangy flavor.

Spinach and Artichoke Stuffed Portobello Mushrooms

Ingredients:

- 4 large portobello mushrooms, stems removed
- 1 tablespoon olive oil
- 1 small onion, finely chopped
- 2 cloves garlic, minced
- 2 cups fresh spinach, chopped
- 1 can (14 oz) artichoke hearts, drained and chopped
- 1/2 cup vegan cream cheese
- 1/4 cup nutritional yeast
- Salt and black pepper to taste
- 1/4 teaspoon red pepper flakes (optional)
- 1/4 cup breadcrumbs (optional, for topping)
- Fresh parsley for garnish

Instructions:

Preheat Oven:
- Preheat the oven to 375°F (190°C).

Prepare Portobello Mushrooms:
- Clean the portobello mushrooms and remove the stems. Place the mushrooms on a baking sheet, gill side up.

Sauté Onion and Garlic:
- In a skillet, heat olive oil over medium heat. Add finely chopped onion and sauté until translucent. Add minced garlic and sauté for an additional 1-2 minutes.

Add Spinach and Artichokes:
- Add chopped spinach and artichoke hearts to the skillet. Cook until the spinach wilts and the artichokes are heated through.

Combine with Cream Cheese:
- Stir in vegan cream cheese and nutritional yeast until well combined. Season with salt, black pepper, and red pepper flakes if using.

Stuff Portobello Mushrooms:
- Spoon the spinach and artichoke mixture into the portobello mushrooms, dividing it evenly among them.

Optional Topping:

- If desired, sprinkle breadcrumbs on top of each stuffed mushroom for a crunchy topping.

Bake:
- Bake in the preheated oven for 20-25 minutes or until the mushrooms are tender.

Garnish and Serve:
- Garnish with fresh parsley and serve the stuffed portobello mushrooms hot.

Enjoy your Spinach and Artichoke Stuffed Portobello Mushrooms!

Tips:

- You can add a sprinkle of vegan parmesan cheese on top before baking for added flavor.
- Adjust the spice level by adding more or less red pepper flakes.
- Serve the stuffed mushrooms as a side dish or with a salad for a complete meal.

BBQ Chickpea Stuffed Sweet Potatoes

Ingredients:

For BBQ Chickpeas:

- 2 cans (15 oz each) chickpeas, drained and rinsed
- 1 cup barbecue sauce
- 1 tablespoon olive oil
- 1 teaspoon smoked paprika
- 1 teaspoon garlic powder
- Salt and black pepper to taste

For Sweet Potatoes:

- 4 medium-sized sweet potatoes
- 1 tablespoon olive oil
- Salt and black pepper to taste

Optional Toppings:

- Vegan coleslaw
- Sliced green onions
- Avocado slices
- Vegan ranch dressing

Instructions:

Prepare BBQ Chickpeas:

    Preheat Oven:
- Preheat the oven to 400°F (200°C).

    Coat Chickpeas:
- In a bowl, toss chickpeas with barbecue sauce, olive oil, smoked paprika, garlic powder, salt, and black pepper until well coated.

    Bake Chickpeas:

- Spread the coated chickpeas on a baking sheet in a single layer. Bake for 25-30 minutes, stirring halfway through, until the chickpeas are crispy.

Prepare Sweet Potatoes:

Roast Sweet Potatoes:
- While the chickpeas are baking, wash and scrub the sweet potatoes. Rub them with olive oil, salt, and black pepper. Place them on a baking sheet and roast for 45-60 minutes or until tender.

Assemble:
- Once the sweet potatoes are done, slice them open and fluff the insides with a fork. Fill each sweet potato with the BBQ chickpeas.

Serve:

Add Toppings:
- Top the stuffed sweet potatoes with vegan coleslaw, sliced green onions, avocado slices, and a drizzle of vegan ranch dressing if desired.

Enjoy your BBQ Chickpea Stuffed Sweet Potatoes!

Tips:

- Feel free to customize the toppings based on your preferences. Other options include vegan cheese, jalapeños, or chopped cilantro.
- Adjust the level of spiciness by adding more or less smoked paprika or using a spicier barbecue sauce.
- These stuffed sweet potatoes make a satisfying and nutritious meal.

Vegan Lentil Sloppy Joes

Ingredients:

- 1 cup dry brown or green lentils, rinsed and drained
- 3 cups vegetable broth
- 1 tablespoon olive oil
- 1 onion, finely chopped
- 2 cloves garlic, minced
- 1 bell pepper, diced
- 1 carrot, grated
- 1 can (14 oz) crushed tomatoes
- 1/4 cup tomato paste
- 2 tablespoons soy sauce or tamari
- 1 tablespoon maple syrup or agave nectar
- 1 teaspoon chili powder
- 1 teaspoon smoked paprika
- 1/2 teaspoon cumin
- 1/2 teaspoon onion powder
- 1/2 teaspoon garlic powder
- Salt and black pepper to taste
- Hamburger buns, for serving

Instructions:

Cook Lentils:
- In a medium saucepan, combine lentils and vegetable broth. Bring to a boil, then reduce heat to low, cover, and simmer for 25-30 minutes or until lentils are tender. Drain any excess liquid.

Sauté Vegetables:
- In a large skillet, heat olive oil over medium heat. Add chopped onion, minced garlic, diced bell pepper, and grated carrot. Sauté until the vegetables are softened.

Add Lentils:
- Add the cooked lentils to the skillet and stir to combine with the sautéed vegetables.

Prepare Sauce:

- In a bowl, whisk together crushed tomatoes, tomato paste, soy sauce, maple syrup, chili powder, smoked paprika, cumin, onion powder, garlic powder, salt, and black pepper.

Combine and Simmer:
- Pour the sauce over the lentil and vegetable mixture. Stir to combine and let it simmer for 15-20 minutes, allowing the flavors to meld. If the mixture becomes too thick, you can add a bit of water.

Adjust Seasoning:
- Taste and adjust the seasoning, adding more salt or spices if needed.

Serve:
- Spoon the vegan lentil sloppy joe mixture onto hamburger buns.

Enjoy your Vegan Lentil Sloppy Joes!

Tips:

- Customize the level of sweetness by adjusting the amount of maple syrup or agave nectar.
- Serve with your favorite toppings like pickles, coleslaw, or vegan cheese.
- Leftover lentil sloppy joe mixture can be stored in the refrigerator for a few days and reheated as needed.

Creamy Cashew Alfredo with Roasted Cherry Tomatoes

Ingredients:

For Creamy Cashew Alfredo:

- 1 cup raw cashews, soaked in water for at least 4 hours or overnight
- 2 cups unsweetened almond milk or vegetable broth
- 3 cloves garlic, minced
- 2 tablespoons nutritional yeast
- 1 tablespoon lemon juice
- 1 teaspoon onion powder
- Salt and black pepper to taste
- 1/4 teaspoon nutmeg (optional)
- 1/4 cup fresh parsley, chopped (for garnish)

For Roasted Cherry Tomatoes:

- 1 pint cherry tomatoes, halved
- 1 tablespoon olive oil
- Salt and black pepper to taste
- 1 teaspoon dried Italian herbs (optional)

For Pasta:

- 16 oz (450g) fettuccine or your favorite pasta

Instructions:

Prepare Creamy Cashew Alfredo:

Drain Cashews:
- After soaking the cashews, drain and rinse them.

Blend Ingredients:
- In a blender, combine soaked cashews, almond milk (or vegetable broth), minced garlic, nutritional yeast, lemon juice, onion powder, salt, black pepper, and nutmeg. Blend until smooth and creamy.

Adjust Consistency:
- If the sauce is too thick, add more almond milk or vegetable broth until you reach your desired consistency.

Roast Cherry Tomatoes:

Preheat Oven:
- Preheat the oven to 400°F (200°C).

Toss Tomatoes:
- In a bowl, toss halved cherry tomatoes with olive oil, salt, black pepper, and dried Italian herbs.

Roast:
- Spread the tomatoes on a baking sheet and roast in the preheated oven for 15-20 minutes or until they are slightly caramelized.

Cook Pasta:

Cook Fettuccine:
- Cook the fettuccine or your favorite pasta according to the package instructions. Drain and set aside.

Assemble:

Combine Sauce and Pasta:
- In a large mixing bowl, combine the cooked pasta with the creamy cashew Alfredo sauce. Toss until the pasta is evenly coated.

Serve:
- Divide the pasta among serving plates. Top with roasted cherry tomatoes and garnish with fresh parsley.

Enjoy your Creamy Cashew Alfredo with Roasted Cherry Tomatoes!

Tips:

- Feel free to add sautéed vegetables or your favorite plant-based protein for additional flavor and nutrition.
- Adjust the seasoning of the cashew Alfredo sauce to suit your taste preferences.
- You can use gluten-free pasta if you prefer a gluten-free version of this dish.

Vegan Pumpkin and Sage Risotto

Ingredients:

- 1 cup Arborio rice
- 2 tablespoons olive oil
- 1 onion, finely chopped
- 2 cloves garlic, minced
- 1/2 cup dry white wine (optional)
- 4 cups vegetable broth, kept warm
- 1 cup pumpkin puree
- 1/2 cup nutritional yeast
- 1 teaspoon dried sage
- Salt and black pepper to taste
- 1/4 cup fresh sage leaves, chopped (for garnish)
- Vegan Parmesan cheese (optional, for serving)

Instructions:

Sauté Onion and Garlic:
- In a large pan, heat olive oil over medium heat. Add finely chopped onion and sauté until translucent. Add minced garlic and cook for an additional minute.

Toast Arborio Rice:
- Add Arborio rice to the pan and toast it for 1-2 minutes, stirring frequently.

Deglaze with Wine (Optional):
- If using white wine, pour it into the pan and stir until the liquid is mostly absorbed.

Add Pumpkin Puree:
- Stir in the pumpkin puree, nutritional yeast, and dried sage.

Begin Adding Broth:
- Begin adding the warm vegetable broth one ladle at a time, stirring frequently. Allow the liquid to be absorbed before adding the next ladle.

Continue Cooking:
- Continue adding broth and stirring until the rice is creamy and cooked to al dente texture. This process may take around 18-20 minutes.

Season:
- Season the risotto with salt and black pepper to taste. Adjust the consistency with more broth if needed.

Finish with Fresh Sage:
- Stir in chopped fresh sage leaves to add a burst of flavor.

Serve:
- Spoon the vegan pumpkin and sage risotto onto plates. Optionally, sprinkle with vegan Parmesan cheese.

Garnish and Enjoy your Vegan Pumpkin and Sage Risotto!

Tips:

- For a richer flavor, you can sauté the Arborio rice in vegan butter instead of olive oil.
- Feel free to add roasted pumpkin cubes or sautéed mushrooms for added texture.
- If you prefer a nuttier flavor, you can toast the Arborio rice for a few additional minutes before adding liquids.

Cilantro Lime Quinoa Salad

Ingredients:

- 1 cup quinoa, rinsed
- 2 cups water or vegetable broth
- 1 can (15 oz) black beans, drained and rinsed
- 1 cup corn kernels (fresh, frozen, or canned)
- 1 red bell pepper, diced
- 1/2 red onion, finely chopped
- 1 cup cherry tomatoes, halved
- 1/4 cup fresh cilantro, chopped
- 1 avocado, diced
- 1/4 cup olive oil
- 3 tablespoons lime juice
- 2 cloves garlic, minced
- 1 teaspoon ground cumin
- Salt and black pepper to taste
- Optional: Jalapeño slices for added spice

Instructions:

Cook Quinoa:
- In a medium saucepan, combine quinoa and water or vegetable broth. Bring to a boil, then reduce heat to low, cover, and simmer for 15-20 minutes or until the quinoa is cooked and the liquid is absorbed. Fluff with a fork and let it cool.

Prepare Veggies:
- In a large mixing bowl, combine black beans, corn, diced red bell pepper, finely chopped red onion, cherry tomatoes, and chopped cilantro.

Make Dressing:
- In a small bowl, whisk together olive oil, lime juice, minced garlic, ground cumin, salt, and black pepper.

Combine Ingredients:
- Add the cooked and cooled quinoa to the bowl of veggies. Pour the dressing over the quinoa and veggies. Toss everything together until well combined.

Add Avocado:

- Gently fold in diced avocado. Be careful not to mash the avocado too much.

Chill (Optional):
- If time allows, refrigerate the quinoa salad for about 30 minutes to let the flavors meld.

Serve:
- Serve the cilantro lime quinoa salad chilled or at room temperature. Optionally, garnish with additional cilantro and jalapeño slices.

Enjoy your Cilantro Lime Quinoa Salad!

Tips:

- Customize the salad by adding other veggies like cucumber, bell pepper, or radishes.
- For added protein, you can include grilled tofu, chickpeas, or shredded chicken.
- Adjust the lime juice and cilantro amounts based on your taste preferences.

Teriyaki Tofu Stir-Fry

Ingredients:

For Teriyaki Sauce:

- 1/4 cup soy sauce
- 2 tablespoons mirin
- 1 tablespoon rice vinegar
- 1 tablespoon maple syrup or agave nectar
- 1 teaspoon sesame oil
- 1 teaspoon cornstarch (optional, to thicken)

For Stir-Fry:

- 1 block extra-firm tofu, pressed and cubed
- 2 tablespoons vegetable oil
- 1 bell pepper, thinly sliced
- 1 carrot, julienned
- 1 cup broccoli florets
- 1 cup snow peas, ends trimmed
- 2 cloves garlic, minced
- 1 tablespoon ginger, minced
- Cooked rice or noodles for serving
- Sesame seeds and green onions for garnish

Instructions:

Prepare Teriyaki Sauce:

Combine Ingredients:
- In a small bowl, whisk together soy sauce, mirin, rice vinegar, maple syrup (or agave nectar), sesame oil, and cornstarch (if using).

Thicken (Optional):
- If you prefer a thicker sauce, heat the mixture in a small saucepan over low heat until it thickens slightly. Set aside.

Prepare Tofu:

- Press Tofu:
  - Press the tofu to remove excess water. Cut the tofu into cubes.
- Sauté Tofu:
  - In a large pan or wok, heat vegetable oil over medium-high heat. Add tofu cubes and cook until all sides are golden brown. Remove tofu from the pan and set aside.

Prepare Stir-Fry:

- Sauté Vegetables:
  - In the same pan, add a bit more oil if needed. Sauté garlic and ginger until fragrant. Add sliced bell pepper, julienned carrot, broccoli florets, and snow peas. Stir-fry until the vegetables are crisp-tender.
- Add Tofu and Sauce:
  - Return the sautéed tofu to the pan with the vegetables. Pour the prepared teriyaki sauce over the tofu and vegetables. Stir to coat everything evenly.
- Finish Cooking:
  - Cook for an additional 2-3 minutes until the sauce thickens and the tofu and vegetables are well-coated.
- Serve:
  - Serve the teriyaki tofu stir-fry over cooked rice or noodles. Garnish with sesame seeds and chopped green onions.
- Enjoy your Teriyaki Tofu Stir-Fry!

Tips:

- You can add other vegetables like mushrooms, baby corn, or water chestnuts to the stir-fry.
- Adjust the sweetness and saltiness of the teriyaki sauce according to your taste.
- For a spicier version, add red pepper flakes or sriracha to the teriyaki sauce.

Vegan Eggplant Parmesan

Ingredients:

For Breaded Eggplant:

- 2 medium-sized eggplants, thinly sliced
- 1 cup all-purpose flour
- 1 cup plant-based milk (such as almond or soy)
- 2 cups breadcrumbs (preferably seasoned)
- Salt and black pepper to taste
- Cooking spray or olive oil for baking

For Assembly:

- 2 cups vegan marinara sauce
- 1 cup vegan mozzarella cheese, shredded
- 1/2 cup vegan Parmesan cheese, grated
- Fresh basil or parsley for garnish

Instructions:

Prepare Breaded Eggplant:

　Preheat Oven:
　- Preheat the oven to 400°F (200°C).

　Slice Eggplant:
　- Slice the eggplants into thin rounds, about 1/4 inch thick.

　Prepare Breading Station:
　- Set up a breading station with three shallow bowls. In one bowl, place the flour. In the second bowl, pour the plant-based milk. In the third bowl, combine breadcrumbs, salt, and black pepper.

　Bread Eggplant Slices:
　- Dip each eggplant slice first in the flour, then in the plant-based milk, and finally in the breadcrumb mixture, ensuring they are well-coated.

　Bake Eggplant:
　- Place the breaded eggplant slices on a baking sheet lined with parchment paper. Lightly spray or brush them with cooking spray or olive oil. Bake for 25-30 minutes or until golden brown and crispy, flipping halfway through.

Assemble Vegan Eggplant Parmesan:

- Layer Marinara Sauce:
    - In a baking dish, spread a thin layer of marinara sauce.
- Arrange Eggplant Slices:
    - Place a layer of baked eggplant slices over the marinara sauce.
- Add Vegan Cheese:
    - Sprinkle a portion of vegan mozzarella and vegan Parmesan over the eggplant layer.
- Repeat Layers:
    - Repeat the process, creating additional layers of marinara sauce, eggplant slices, and vegan cheese until all ingredients are used. Finish with a layer of vegan cheese on top.
- Bake:
    - Bake in the preheated oven for 20-25 minutes or until the cheese is melted and bubbly.
- Garnish:
    - Remove from the oven and let it rest for a few minutes. Garnish with fresh basil or parsley.
- Serve:
    - Serve the vegan eggplant Parmesan with your favorite side, such as pasta or a green salad.
- Enjoy your Vegan Eggplant Parmesan!

Tips:

- Ensure the eggplant slices are evenly coated with breadcrumbs for a crispy texture.
- If you prefer, you can pan-fry the breaded eggplant slices instead of baking them.
- Feel free to customize the marinara sauce with your favorite herbs and spices.

Coconut Curry Chickpea Stew

Ingredients:

- 2 tablespoons coconut oil
- 1 large onion, finely chopped
- 3 cloves garlic, minced
- 1 tablespoon fresh ginger, grated
- 1 tablespoon curry powder
- 1 teaspoon ground cumin
- 1 teaspoon ground coriander
- 1 teaspoon turmeric
- 1/2 teaspoon chili powder (adjust to taste)
- 1 can (14 oz) diced tomatoes
- 1 can (14 oz) chickpeas, drained and rinsed
- 1 can (14 oz) coconut milk
- 2 cups vegetable broth
- 1 sweet potato, peeled and diced
- 1 cup cauliflower florets
- 1 cup baby spinach
- Salt and black pepper to taste
- Fresh cilantro, chopped (for garnish)
- Cooked rice or naan (for serving)

Instructions:

Sauté Aromatics:
- In a large pot, heat coconut oil over medium heat. Add chopped onion, minced garlic, and grated ginger. Sauté until the onion is translucent.

Add Spices:
- Add curry powder, ground cumin, ground coriander, turmeric, and chili powder. Stir and cook for 1-2 minutes to toast the spices.

Add Tomatoes:
- Pour in the diced tomatoes with their juices. Stir to combine.

Simmer Chickpeas:
- Add the drained and rinsed chickpeas to the pot. Allow the mixture to simmer for 5 minutes.

Pour Coconut Milk and Broth:

- Pour in the coconut milk and vegetable broth. Stir well to combine.

Add Vegetables:
- Add diced sweet potato and cauliflower florets to the pot. Bring the stew to a simmer, then reduce the heat and let it cook for about 15-20 minutes or until the vegetables are tender.

Stir in Spinach:
- Add baby spinach to the stew and stir until wilted.

Season:
- Season the stew with salt and black pepper to taste. Adjust the spice level if needed.

Serve:
- Ladle the coconut curry chickpea stew over cooked rice or alongside naan.

Garnish:
- Garnish with chopped fresh cilantro.

Enjoy your Coconut Curry Chickpea Stew!

Tips:

- Customize the vegetables based on your preferences. You can add bell peppers, peas, or any other favorite veggies.
- Adjust the spice levels by increasing or decreasing the amount of chili powder.
- If you prefer a creamier texture, you can use full-fat coconut milk.

Vegan Broccoli and Cheese Stuffed Baked Potatoes

Ingredients:

For Baked Potatoes:

- 4 large russet potatoes, scrubbed
- 1 tablespoon olive oil
- Salt and black pepper to taste

For Broccoli and Cheese Filling:

- 2 cups broccoli florets, steamed or boiled
- 1 cup vegan cheddar cheese, shredded
- 1/2 cup unsweetened almond milk (or any plant-based milk)
- 2 tablespoons nutritional yeast
- 1 tablespoon cornstarch
- 1 teaspoon Dijon mustard
- 1/2 teaspoon garlic powder
- Salt and black pepper to taste

Optional Toppings:

- Vegan sour cream
- Chopped chives or green onions

Instructions:

Bake Potatoes:

    Preheat Oven:
- Preheat the oven to 400°F (200°C).

    Prepare Potatoes:
- Rub the scrubbed potatoes with olive oil, then sprinkle with salt and black pepper. Place them on a baking sheet.

    Bake:
- Bake the potatoes in the preheated oven for about 45-60 minutes or until they are tender when pierced with a fork.

Prepare Broccoli and Cheese Filling:

Steam or Boil Broccoli:
- Steam or boil the broccoli until it's just tender. Drain and set aside.

Make Cheese Sauce:
- In a saucepan, whisk together almond milk, nutritional yeast, cornstarch, Dijon mustard, garlic powder, salt, and black pepper over medium heat. Stir constantly until the mixture thickens.

Add Vegan Cheese:
- Once thickened, stir in the vegan cheddar cheese until it melts and the sauce is smooth.

Combine Broccoli and Cheese:
- Add the steamed broccoli to the cheese sauce. Stir to coat the broccoli evenly.

Assemble Broccoli and Cheese Stuffed Baked Potatoes:

Slice Potatoes:
- Once the baked potatoes are done, let them cool slightly, then slice them open lengthwise.

Fluff Potato Flesh:
- Gently fluff the insides of the potatoes with a fork.

Fill Potatoes:
- Spoon the broccoli and cheese mixture into each baked potato, distributing it evenly.

Optional:
- Top each stuffed potato with a dollop of vegan sour cream and sprinkle with chopped chives or green onions.

Serve:
- Serve the vegan broccoli and cheese stuffed baked potatoes while warm.

Enjoy your Vegan Broccoli and Cheese Stuffed Baked Potatoes!

Tips:

- Feel free to add other toppings like sliced avocado, hot sauce, or vegan bacon bits.
- Adjust the thickness of the cheese sauce by adding more or less almond milk.
- You can prepare the cheese sauce ahead of time and reheat it when ready to assemble the stuffed potatoes.

Spaghetti Aglio e Olio with Roasted Vegetables

Ingredients:

- 1 pound (450g) spaghetti
- 1/3 cup olive oil
- 6 cloves garlic, thinly sliced
- 1 teaspoon red pepper flakes (adjust to taste)
- Zest of 1 lemon
- Salt to taste
- Black pepper to taste
- 1 cup cherry tomatoes, halved
- 1 zucchini, thinly sliced
- 1 bell pepper, thinly sliced
- 1/4 cup fresh parsley, chopped
- Vegan Parmesan or nutritional yeast for serving (optional)

Instructions:

Roast Vegetables:

Preheat Oven:
- Preheat the oven to 400°F (200°C).

Prepare Vegetables:
- Place the halved cherry tomatoes, sliced zucchini, and sliced bell pepper on a baking sheet. Drizzle with olive oil, salt, and pepper. Toss to coat the vegetables evenly.

Roast:
- Roast the vegetables in the preheated oven for 20-25 minutes or until they are tender and slightly caramelized. Set aside.

Cook Spaghetti:

Boil Water:
- Bring a large pot of salted water to a boil.

Cook Spaghetti:
- Cook the spaghetti according to the package instructions until al dente. Reserve about 1 cup of pasta cooking water before draining.

Prepare Aglio e Olio Sauce:

Sauté Garlic:
- While the pasta is cooking, heat 1/3 cup of olive oil in a large skillet over medium heat. Add the thinly sliced garlic and red pepper flakes. Sauté until the garlic is golden but not browned.

Zest Lemon:
- Add the lemon zest to the skillet and stir to combine.

Combine Pasta, Sauce, and Vegetables:

Drain Pasta:
- Drain the cooked spaghetti and add it to the skillet with the aglio e olio sauce. Toss to coat the pasta evenly.

Add Roasted Vegetables:
- Add the roasted cherry tomatoes, zucchini, and bell pepper to the pasta. Toss gently to combine.

Adjust Seasoning:
- Season with salt and black pepper to taste. If the pasta seems dry, add some of the reserved pasta cooking water to create a silky sauce.

Serve:

Garnish:
- Garnish with chopped fresh parsley and, if desired, vegan Parmesan or nutritional yeast.

Serve Warm:
- Serve the Spaghetti Aglio e Olio with Roasted Vegetables immediately.

Enjoy your flavorful and veggie-packed pasta dish!

Tips:

- Feel free to add other roasted vegetables like asparagus, mushrooms, or eggplant.
- Adjust the level of red pepper flakes based on your spice preference.
- Use high-quality olive oil for the best flavor in the aglio e olio sauce.

Moroccan Chickpea and Vegetable Tagine

Ingredients:

- 2 tablespoons olive oil
- 1 large onion, finely chopped
- 3 cloves garlic, minced
- 1 teaspoon ground cumin
- 1 teaspoon ground coriander
- 1 teaspoon ground cinnamon
- 1 teaspoon ground turmeric
- 1 teaspoon paprika
- 1/2 teaspoon cayenne pepper (adjust to taste)
- 1 can (14 oz) chickpeas, drained and rinsed
- 2 carrots, peeled and diced
- 1 zucchini, diced
- 1 bell pepper, diced
- 1 can (14 oz) diced tomatoes
- 1 cup vegetable broth
- 1 cup butternut squash, diced
- 1/2 cup dried apricots, chopped
- Salt and black pepper to taste
- Fresh cilantro or parsley for garnish
- Cooked couscous or rice for serving

Instructions:

Sauté Aromatics:
- In a large tagine or a deep skillet, heat olive oil over medium heat. Add chopped onions and sauté until they become translucent.

Add Spices:
- Add minced garlic, ground cumin, ground coriander, ground cinnamon, ground turmeric, paprika, and cayenne pepper. Stir well and cook for about 1-2 minutes until fragrant.

Add Vegetables and Chickpeas:
- Add diced carrots, zucchini, bell pepper, chickpeas, and stir to coat them in the spices.

Pour in Tomatoes and Broth:

- Pour in the diced tomatoes with their juices and vegetable broth. Stir to combine.

Add Butternut Squash and Apricots:
- Add diced butternut squash and chopped dried apricots to the tagine. Mix well.

Simmer:
- Bring the mixture to a simmer, then reduce the heat to low. Cover the tagine and let it simmer for 20-25 minutes or until the vegetables are tender.

Season:
- Season with salt and black pepper to taste. Adjust the spices if needed.

Garnish and Serve:
- Garnish the Moroccan Chickpea and Vegetable Tagine with fresh cilantro or parsley. Serve it over cooked couscous or rice.

Enjoy your flavorful and aromatic Moroccan tagine!

Tips:

- Customize the vegetables based on what you have or your preferences.
- Adjust the level of cayenne pepper for spiciness according to your taste.
- You can add a handful of green olives for a briny flavor.

Vegan Sushi Rolls

Ingredients:

For Sushi Rice:

- 2 cups sushi rice
- 2 1/2 cups water
- 1/2 cup rice vinegar
- 3 tablespoons sugar
- 1 teaspoon salt

For Vegan Sushi Rolls:

- Nori (seaweed) sheets
- Sushi rice
- Avocado, sliced
- Carrots, julienned
- Cucumber, julienned
- Bell peppers, thinly sliced
- Tofu, thinly sliced and sautéed or marinated
- Soy sauce or tamari (for dipping)
- Pickled ginger (for serving)
- Wasabi (for serving)
- Sesame seeds (for garnish)
- Bamboo sushi rolling mat

Instructions:

Prepare Sushi Rice:

Rinse Rice:
- Rinse sushi rice under cold water until the water runs clear.

Cook Rice:
- In a rice cooker or on the stovetop, cook the sushi rice with water according to the package instructions.

Prepare Seasoning:

- In a small saucepan, combine rice vinegar, sugar, and salt. Heat over low heat until the sugar and salt dissolve. Let it cool.

Season Rice:
- Once the rice is cooked, transfer it to a large bowl. Gradually add the seasoned vinegar mixture, gently folding it into the rice. Let the rice cool to room temperature.

Assemble Vegan Sushi Rolls:

Prepare Ingredients:
- Prepare all your vegetables, tofu, and other fillings by slicing or julienning them.

Place Nori on Mat:
- Lay a sheet of nori on the bamboo sushi rolling mat, shiny side down.

Spread Sushi Rice:
- Wet your hands and spread a thin layer of sushi rice over the nori, leaving a small border at the top.

Add Fillings:
- Arrange your desired fillings (avocado, carrots, cucumber, tofu, etc.) in the center of the rice.

Roll the Sushi:
- Using the bamboo mat, carefully roll the sushi away from you, applying gentle pressure. Seal the edge with a bit of water.

Slice Rolls:
- With a sharp knife dipped in water, slice the roll into bite-sized pieces.

Repeat:
- Repeat the process with the remaining ingredients.

Serve:
- Arrange the vegan sushi rolls on a plate. Sprinkle with sesame seeds and serve with soy sauce, pickled ginger, and wasabi.

Enjoy your homemade Vegan Sushi Rolls!

Tips:

- Be creative with your fillings! You can add ingredients like mango, asparagus, or marinated mushrooms.
- Use a bamboo sushi rolling mat for easier rolling.
- Wet your knife before each slice to get clean cuts.

Vegan Buffalo Cauliflower Bites

Ingredients:

- 1 head cauliflower, cut into florets
- 1 cup all-purpose flour
- 1 cup plant-based milk (such as almond, soy, or oat milk)
- 1 teaspoon garlic powder
- 1 teaspoon onion powder
- 1/2 teaspoon smoked paprika
- 1/2 teaspoon salt
- 1/4 teaspoon black pepper
- 1 cup breadcrumbs (preferably panko)
- 1 cup buffalo sauce (store-bought or homemade)
- 2 tablespoons melted vegan butter
- Fresh parsley or cilantro, chopped (for garnish, optional)
- Vegan ranch or blue cheese dressing (for dipping)

Instructions:

Preheat Oven:
- Preheat your oven to 450°F (230°C). Line a baking sheet with parchment paper.

Prepare Batter:
- In a bowl, whisk together the flour, plant-based milk, garlic powder, onion powder, smoked paprika, salt, and black pepper to create a smooth batter.

Coat Cauliflower:
- Dip each cauliflower floret into the batter, ensuring it's fully coated.

Breadcrumb Coating:
- Roll the battered cauliflower in breadcrumbs, pressing the breadcrumbs onto the florets to adhere.

Bake:
- Place the coated cauliflower on the prepared baking sheet. Bake in the preheated oven for 20-25 minutes or until golden and crispy, flipping halfway through.

Prepare Buffalo Sauce:
- While the cauliflower is baking, mix together the buffalo sauce and melted vegan butter in a bowl.

Coat in Buffalo Sauce:

- Once the cauliflower is done baking, transfer it to a large bowl. Pour the buffalo sauce mixture over the baked cauliflower and toss until each piece is well-coated.

Serve:
- Arrange the buffalo cauliflower bites on a serving platter. Garnish with chopped parsley or cilantro if desired.

Dip and Enjoy:
- Serve the vegan buffalo cauliflower bites with vegan ranch or blue cheese dressing for dipping.

Enjoy your Vegan Buffalo Cauliflower Bites!

Tips:

- Adjust the level of spiciness by adding more or less buffalo sauce.
- For extra crispiness, you can use an air fryer to cook the cauliflower bites instead of baking.
- Feel free to customize the batter by adding your favorite spices or herbs.

Ratatouille with Herbed Polenta

Ingredients:

For Ratatouille:

- 1 eggplant, diced
- 2 zucchinis, diced
- 1 yellow bell pepper, diced
- 1 red bell pepper, diced
- 1 onion, diced
- 3 cloves garlic, minced
- 2 cups tomatoes, diced (fresh or canned)
- 1/4 cup tomato paste
- 2 tablespoons olive oil
- 1 teaspoon dried thyme
- 1 teaspoon dried rosemary
- 1 teaspoon dried oregano
- Salt and pepper to taste
- Fresh basil or parsley for garnish

For Herbed Polenta:

- 1 cup polenta (cornmeal)
- 4 cups vegetable broth
- 2 tablespoons vegan butter
- 1 teaspoon dried thyme
- Salt and pepper to taste

Instructions:

Prepare Ratatouille:

    Sauté Aromatics:
- In a large pot or Dutch oven, heat olive oil over medium heat. Add diced onion and minced garlic. Sauté until the onion becomes translucent.

    Add Vegetables:
- Add diced eggplant, zucchinis, yellow and red bell peppers to the pot. Cook for 5-7 minutes until the vegetables start to soften.

    Stir in Tomatoes and Paste:

- Stir in diced tomatoes and tomato paste. Mix well.

Season:
- Add dried thyme, dried rosemary, dried oregano, salt, and pepper. Stir to combine. Allow the mixture to simmer for about 20-25 minutes or until the vegetables are tender.

Garnish:
- Just before serving, garnish the ratatouille with fresh basil or parsley.

Prepare Herbed Polenta:

Boil Broth:
- In a separate pot, bring vegetable broth to a boil.

Whisk in Polenta:
- Gradually whisk in the polenta, stirring continuously to avoid lumps.

Cook Polenta:
- Reduce the heat to low and let the polenta simmer, stirring often, until it thickens and becomes creamy.

Add Herbs and Butter:
- Stir in dried thyme, vegan butter, salt, and pepper. Continue to cook until the polenta is smooth and creamy.

Serve:
- Spoon the herbed polenta onto plates or into bowls. Top it with a generous serving of ratatouille.

Garnish:
- Garnish with additional fresh herbs if desired.

Enjoy your Ratatouille with Herbed Polenta!

Tips:

- Feel free to add other vegetables like cherry tomatoes or mushrooms to the ratatouille.
- Adjust the seasoning according to your taste preferences.
- You can sprinkle vegan cheese on top of the polenta for added flavor.

Creamy Vegan Tomato Basil Soup

Ingredients:

- 1 tablespoon olive oil
- 1 onion, chopped
- 3 cloves garlic, minced
- 1 can (28 oz) whole peeled tomatoes
- 1 can (14 oz) diced tomatoes
- 1 can (14 oz) coconut milk (full-fat)
- 1 cup vegetable broth
- 2 tablespoons tomato paste
- 1 teaspoon dried basil
- 1 teaspoon dried oregano
- 1/2 teaspoon dried thyme
- Salt and pepper to taste
- 1/4 cup fresh basil, chopped (for garnish)
- Croutons or bread (for serving, optional)

Instructions:

Sauté Aromatics:
- In a large pot, heat olive oil over medium heat. Add chopped onion and sauté until it becomes translucent.

Add Garlic:
- Add minced garlic to the pot and sauté for an additional 1-2 minutes until fragrant.

Combine Tomatoes:
- Add both cans of tomatoes (whole peeled and diced) to the pot. Break up the whole tomatoes with a spoon.

Add Coconut Milk and Broth:
- Pour in the coconut milk and vegetable broth. Stir well to combine.

Stir in Tomato Paste:
- Add tomato paste to the soup for extra richness and flavor. Stir until well incorporated.

Season:
- Add dried basil, dried oregano, dried thyme, salt, and pepper. Stir and let the soup simmer for about 15-20 minutes to allow the flavors to meld.

Blend the Soup:

- Using an immersion blender, blend the soup until smooth and creamy. Alternatively, transfer the soup to a blender in batches and blend until smooth. Be cautious as hot soup can splatter.

Adjust Consistency:
- If the soup is too thick, you can add more vegetable broth to reach your desired consistency.

Check Seasoning:
- Taste the soup and adjust the seasoning if needed.

Serve:
- Ladle the creamy vegan tomato basil soup into bowls. Garnish with fresh chopped basil.

Optional:
- Serve with croutons or a slice of bread on the side.

Enjoy your Creamy Vegan Tomato Basil Soup!

Tips:

- For an extra creamy texture, use full-fat coconut milk.
- Customize the soup by adding a pinch of red pepper flakes for a hint of heat.
- If using fresh tomatoes, blanch and peel them before adding to the soup.

Chickpea and Spinach Coconut Curry

Ingredients:

- 1 tablespoon coconut oil
- 1 onion, finely chopped
- 3 cloves garlic, minced
- 1 tablespoon ginger, grated
- 1 tablespoon curry powder
- 1 teaspoon ground cumin
- 1 teaspoon ground coriander
- 1 teaspoon turmeric
- 1 can (15 oz) chickpeas, drained and rinsed
- 1 can (14 oz) diced tomatoes
- 1 can (14 oz) coconut milk (full-fat)
- 4 cups fresh spinach, washed and chopped
- Salt and pepper to taste
- Fresh cilantro, chopped (for garnish)
- Cooked rice or naan (for serving)

Instructions:

Sauté Aromatics:
- In a large pan or pot, heat coconut oil over medium heat. Add chopped onion and sauté until it becomes translucent.

Add Garlic and Ginger:
- Add minced garlic and grated ginger to the pan. Sauté for an additional 1-2 minutes until fragrant.

Spice Mixture:
- Stir in curry powder, ground cumin, ground coriander, and turmeric. Cook for 1-2 minutes to toast the spices.

Chickpeas and Tomatoes:
- Add drained chickpeas and diced tomatoes (with their juices) to the pan. Stir to combine.

Pour Coconut Milk:
- Pour in the coconut milk. Stir well and bring the mixture to a simmer. Let it cook for 10-15 minutes, allowing the flavors to meld.

Add Spinach:

- Add chopped fresh spinach to the curry. Stir until the spinach wilts and cooks down.

Season:
- Season the curry with salt and pepper to taste. Adjust the seasoning according to your preferences.

Garnish:
- Garnish the chickpea and spinach coconut curry with fresh cilantro.

Serve:
- Serve the curry over cooked rice or with naan bread.

Enjoy your Chickpea and Spinach Coconut Curry!

Tips:

- Customize the spice level by adjusting the amount of curry powder and adding chili powder or red pepper flakes.
- You can add other vegetables like bell peppers, peas, or carrots for extra flavor and nutrition.
- Experiment with different types of curry paste or add a squeeze of lime for a citrusy kick.

Vegan Stuffed Bell Peppers

Ingredients:

- 4 large bell peppers (any color)
- 1 cup quinoa, cooked
- 1 can (15 oz) black beans, drained and rinsed
- 1 cup corn kernels (fresh or frozen)
- 1 cup tomatoes, diced
- 1/2 cup red onion, finely chopped
- 1/2 cup fresh cilantro, chopped
- 2 cloves garlic, minced
- 1 teaspoon ground cumin
- 1 teaspoon chili powder
- 1/2 teaspoon smoked paprika
- Salt and pepper to taste
- 1 cup tomato sauce or salsa
- 1 cup vegan shredded cheese
- Avocado slices (for garnish, optional)
- Fresh cilantro or green onions (for garnish, optional)

Instructions:

Preheat Oven:
- Preheat your oven to 375°F (190°C).

Prepare Bell Peppers:
- Cut the tops off the bell peppers and remove the seeds and membranes. Lightly brush the outside of the peppers with oil.

Cook Quinoa:
- Cook quinoa according to package instructions.

Prepare Filling:
- In a large mixing bowl, combine cooked quinoa, black beans, corn, diced tomatoes, red onion, cilantro, minced garlic, ground cumin, chili powder, smoked paprika, salt, and pepper. Mix well.

Stuff Bell Peppers:
- Stuff each bell pepper with the quinoa mixture, pressing it down to pack the filling.

Top with Sauce and Cheese:

- Pour tomato sauce or salsa over the stuffed peppers. Top each pepper with a generous amount of vegan shredded cheese.

Bake:
- Place the stuffed peppers in a baking dish. Bake in the preheated oven for 25-30 minutes or until the peppers are tender and the cheese is melted and bubbly.

Garnish:
- Remove from the oven and garnish with avocado slices, fresh cilantro, or green onions if desired.

Serve:
- Serve the vegan stuffed bell peppers hot, and enjoy!

Tips:

- You can add other vegetables like chopped spinach or mushrooms to the filling.
- Experiment with different types of vegan cheese for varied flavors.
- Serve with a side of guacamole or vegan sour cream for extra creaminess.

Mexican Street Corn Salad

Ingredients:

- 4 cups corn kernels (fresh or frozen, cooked)
- 1/2 cup vegan mayonnaise
- 1/4 cup vegan sour cream
- 1/4 cup fresh cilantro, chopped
- 1/4 cup green onions, chopped
- 1/2 cup red onion, finely chopped
- 1 clove garlic, minced
- 1 teaspoon chili powder
- 1/2 teaspoon cumin
- Juice of 1 lime
- Salt and pepper to taste
- 1 cup vegan feta or cotija cheese, crumbled (optional)
- Lime wedges and additional cilantro for garnish

Instructions:

Cook Corn:
- If using fresh corn, grill or boil the corn until it's cooked. If using frozen corn, cook it according to the package instructions. Allow the corn to cool.

Prepare Dressing:
- In a large bowl, whisk together vegan mayonnaise, vegan sour cream, chopped cilantro, green onions, red onion, minced garlic, chili powder, cumin, lime juice, salt, and pepper.

Combine with Corn:
- Add the cooked corn to the dressing mixture. Toss until the corn is well-coated with the dressing.

Chill:
- Refrigerate the Mexican Street Corn Salad for at least 30 minutes to allow the flavors to meld.

Garnish:
- Just before serving, garnish with crumbled vegan feta or cotija cheese if desired.

Serve:

- Serve the Mexican Street Corn Salad chilled, garnished with lime wedges and additional cilantro.

Enjoy your Mexican Street Corn Salad!

Tips:

- If you prefer a spicier version, you can add a pinch of cayenne pepper or hot sauce to the dressing.
- Grilling the corn adds a smoky flavor to the salad.
- Adjust the lime juice, salt, and pepper according to your taste preferences.

Vegan Black Bean Burgers

Ingredients:

- 2 cans (15 oz each) black beans, drained and rinsed
- 1 cup breadcrumbs (whole wheat or gluten-free)
- 1/2 cup finely chopped red onion
- 1/2 cup finely chopped bell pepper (any color)
- 2 cloves garlic, minced
- 1 tablespoon ground flaxseed mixed with 3 tablespoons water (flax egg)
- 1 tablespoon soy sauce or tamari
- 1 teaspoon cumin
- 1 teaspoon chili powder
- 1/2 teaspoon smoked paprika
- Salt and pepper to taste
- 1/4 cup fresh cilantro or parsley, chopped
- 1 tablespoon olive oil (for cooking)
- Burger buns and desired toppings (lettuce, tomato, vegan mayo, etc.)

Instructions:

Prepare Flax Egg:
- In a small bowl, mix ground flaxseed with water and set aside to thicken, creating a flax egg.

Mash Black Beans:
- In a large bowl, partially mash black beans with a fork or potato masher. Leave some beans whole for texture.

Add Ingredients:
- Add breadcrumbs, chopped red onion, chopped bell pepper, minced garlic, flax egg, soy sauce, cumin, chili powder, smoked paprika, salt, pepper, and chopped cilantro or parsley to the mashed black beans.

Mix Thoroughly:
- Mix the ingredients thoroughly until well combined. The mixture should be sticky enough to form into patties.

Form Patties:
- Divide the mixture into equal portions and shape into burger patties. If the mixture is too wet, add more breadcrumbs.

Chill Patties:

- Place the formed patties in the refrigerator for at least 30 minutes to firm up.

Cook Burgers:
- Heat olive oil in a skillet over medium heat. Cook the black bean burgers for 4-5 minutes on each side or until they are golden brown and cooked through.

Serve:
- Toast burger buns, if desired. Assemble the black bean burgers with your favorite toppings.

Enjoy your Vegan Black Bean Burgers!

Tips:

- For added flavor, you can add a dash of hot sauce or your favorite spices to the burger mixture.
- If the mixture is too dry, you can add a bit of water or vegetable broth.
- Grill the burgers for a smoky flavor or bake them in the oven for a healthier option.

Lemon Garlic Roasted Brussels Sprouts

Ingredients:

- 1 pound Brussels sprouts, trimmed and halved
- 3 tablespoons olive oil
- 3 cloves garlic, minced
- Zest of 1 lemon
- Juice of 1 lemon
- 1 teaspoon Dijon mustard
- Salt and pepper to taste
- Red pepper flakes (optional, for a bit of heat)
- Fresh parsley, chopped (for garnish)

Instructions:

Preheat Oven:
- Preheat your oven to 400°F (200°C).

Prepare Brussels Sprouts:
- Trim the ends of the Brussels sprouts and cut them in half.

Make the Marinade:
- In a bowl, whisk together olive oil, minced garlic, lemon zest, lemon juice, Dijon mustard, salt, pepper, and red pepper flakes if using.

Coat Brussels Sprouts:
- Toss the halved Brussels sprouts in the marinade until they are well coated.

Roast in the Oven:
- Spread the Brussels sprouts evenly on a baking sheet lined with parchment paper. Roast in the preheated oven for 25-30 minutes or until they are golden brown and crispy on the edges. Stir or shake the pan halfway through to ensure even roasting.

Garnish:
- Remove from the oven and garnish with fresh chopped parsley.

Serve:
- Transfer the lemon garlic roasted Brussels sprouts to a serving dish and serve immediately.

Enjoy your Lemon Garlic Roasted Brussels Sprouts!

Tips:

- For an extra kick, you can add a pinch of red pepper flakes to the marinade.
- Adjust the lemon juice and zest according to your taste preferences.
- Serve with a wedge of lemon on the side for an extra burst of citrus flavor.

Vegan Chocolate Avocado Mousse

Ingredients:

- 2 ripe avocados, peeled and pitted
- 1/2 cup cocoa powder
- 1/2 cup maple syrup or agave nectar
- 1 teaspoon vanilla extract
- Pinch of salt
- 1/4 cup almond milk or any plant-based milk

Optional Toppings:

- Fresh berries
- Nuts or seeds (e.g., chopped almonds or chia seeds)
- Vegan whipped cream

Instructions:

Prepare Avocados:
- Scoop the flesh of the ripe avocados into a blender or food processor.

Add Cocoa Powder:
- Add cocoa powder to the blender.

Sweeten with Maple Syrup:
- Pour in the maple syrup or agave nectar for sweetness.

Add Vanilla and Salt:
- Add vanilla extract and a pinch of salt to enhance the flavors.

Blend Until Smooth:
- Blend all the ingredients until smooth and creamy. You may need to stop and scrape down the sides of the blender to ensure everything is well mixed.

Adjust Consistency:
- If the mixture is too thick, add almond milk (or any plant-based milk) a little at a time until you achieve the desired consistency.

Chill:
- Transfer the chocolate avocado mousse to serving bowls or glasses. Chill in the refrigerator for at least 1-2 hours before serving.

Add Toppings:

- Before serving, top the chocolate avocado mousse with fresh berries, chopped nuts or seeds, and vegan whipped cream if desired.

Enjoy your Vegan Chocolate Avocado Mousse!

Tips:

- Adjust the sweetness by adding more or less maple syrup/agave according to your taste.
- For a richer flavor, you can add a small amount of instant coffee or espresso powder.
- Experiment with toppings like shredded coconut or a sprinkle of cocoa nibs for added texture.

Vegan Caesar Salad with Crispy Chickpea Croutons

Ingredients:

For the Caesar Dressing:

- 1/2 cup raw cashews, soaked in hot water for 1-2 hours or overnight
- 2 tablespoons nutritional yeast
- 2 tablespoons lemon juice
- 1 tablespoon Dijon mustard
- 2 cloves garlic, minced
- 1 teaspoon capers
- 1 teaspoon white miso paste (optional)
- 1/2 cup water
- Salt and pepper to taste

For the Crispy Chickpea Croutons:

- 1 can (15 oz) chickpeas, drained and rinsed
- 1 tablespoon olive oil
- 1 teaspoon smoked paprika
- 1/2 teaspoon garlic powder
- Salt and pepper to taste

For the Salad:

- Romaine lettuce, chopped
- Cherry tomatoes, halved
- Red onion, thinly sliced
- Vegan parmesan cheese, grated
- Lemon wedges (for serving)

Instructions:

For the Caesar Dressing:

    Drain Cashews:
- After soaking the cashews, drain and rinse them.

    Blend Ingredients:

- In a blender, combine soaked cashews, nutritional yeast, lemon juice, Dijon mustard, minced garlic, capers, miso paste (if using), water, salt, and pepper. Blend until smooth and creamy.

Adjust Consistency:
- If the dressing is too thick, you can add more water to reach your desired consistency. Adjust salt and pepper to taste.

For the Crispy Chickpea Croutons:

Preheat Oven:
- Preheat your oven to 400°F (200°C).

Dry Chickpeas:
- Pat the chickpeas dry with a kitchen towel to remove excess moisture.

Season and Roast:
- In a bowl, toss chickpeas with olive oil, smoked paprika, garlic powder, salt, and pepper. Spread them on a baking sheet in a single layer. Roast for 25-30 minutes or until crispy, shaking the pan halfway through.

For the Salad:

Assemble Salad:
- In a large bowl, combine chopped Romaine lettuce, halved cherry tomatoes, thinly sliced red onion, and grated vegan parmesan cheese.

Add Dressing and Croutons:
- Drizzle the Caesar dressing over the salad and toss to coat. Top the salad with crispy chickpea croutons.

Serve:
- Serve the Vegan Caesar Salad with lemon wedges on the side.

Enjoy your Vegan Caesar Salad with Crispy Chickpea Croutons!

Tips:

- Make extra crispy chickpea croutons as they make a delicious snack on their own.
- Adjust the dressing consistency with more or less water according to your preference.
- Feel free to customize the salad with your favorite veggies or add protein sources like grilled tofu or tempeh.

Vegan Thai Green Curry

Ingredients:

For the Green Curry Paste:

- 2 green Thai chilies, chopped (adjust to taste for spice level)
- 2 stalks lemongrass, sliced (use only the tender inner part)
- 1 small shallot, chopped
- 4 cloves garlic, minced
- 1 thumb-sized piece of ginger, peeled and sliced
- 1 bunch fresh cilantro, stems and leaves
- 1 teaspoon ground coriander
- 1 teaspoon ground cumin
- 1/2 teaspoon white pepper
- Zest of 1 lime
- 2 tablespoons soy sauce or tamari
- 1 tablespoon agave nectar or maple syrup
- 2 tablespoons vegetable oil

For the Green Curry:

- 1 tablespoon vegetable oil
- 1 can (14 oz) coconut milk
- 1 cup vegetable broth
- 1 block (14 oz) firm tofu, cubed
- 1 cup broccoli florets
- 1 bell pepper, sliced
- 1 zucchini, sliced
- 1 carrot, sliced
- 1 cup snap peas, trimmed
- Fresh basil or Thai basil leaves (for garnish)
- Cooked jasmine rice (for serving)

Instructions:

For the Green Curry Paste:

    Prepare Ingredients:
- In a food processor, combine all the green curry paste ingredients.

Blend into Paste:
- Blend until a smooth paste is formed. You may need to scrape down the sides of the food processor to ensure everything is well combined.

For the Green Curry:

Sauté Curry Paste:
- Heat vegetable oil in a large pot over medium heat. Add the green curry paste and sauté for 2-3 minutes until fragrant.

Add Coconut Milk:
- Pour in the coconut milk and vegetable broth. Stir well to combine.

Add Tofu and Vegetables:
- Add cubed tofu, broccoli, bell pepper, zucchini, carrot, and snap peas to the pot. Simmer for 15-20 minutes or until the vegetables are tender.

Adjust Seasoning:
- Taste the curry and adjust the seasoning with more soy sauce, agave nectar (or maple syrup), or lime juice as needed.

Serve:
- Serve the Vegan Thai Green Curry over cooked jasmine rice. Garnish with fresh basil or Thai basil leaves.

Enjoy your Vegan Thai Green Curry!

Tips:

- Adjust the quantity of green Thai chilies according to your spice preference.
- You can customize the vegetables based on your liking or what's in season.
- For added protein, you can add chickpeas, tempeh, or your favorite plant-based protein source.

Sweet and Spicy Glazed Tempeh

Ingredients:

- 1 block (8 oz) tempeh, cut into cubes or strips
- 2 tablespoons soy sauce or tamari
- 2 tablespoons maple syrup or agave nectar
- 1 tablespoon rice vinegar
- 1 tablespoon sriracha sauce (adjust to taste)
- 1 tablespoon tomato paste
- 2 cloves garlic, minced
- 1 teaspoon grated ginger
- 1 tablespoon vegetable oil
- Sesame seeds and chopped green onions (for garnish)
- Cooked rice or quinoa (for serving)

Instructions:

Prepare Tempeh:
- Steam the tempeh for 10 minutes to reduce its bitterness. Allow it to cool, then cut it into cubes or strips.

Make the Glaze:
- In a bowl, whisk together soy sauce, maple syrup, rice vinegar, sriracha sauce, tomato paste, minced garlic, and grated ginger to create the glaze.

Marinate Tempeh:
- Place the tempeh cubes/strips in a shallow dish and pour half of the glaze over them. Allow it to marinate for at least 15-20 minutes.

Cook Tempeh:
- Heat vegetable oil in a skillet over medium heat. Add the marinated tempeh and cook for 2-3 minutes on each side until golden brown.

Add Remaining Glaze:
- Pour the remaining glaze over the cooking tempeh. Allow it to simmer and coat the tempeh until the glaze thickens and becomes sticky.

Garnish and Serve:
- Garnish the sweet and spicy glazed tempeh with sesame seeds and chopped green onions.

Serve:
- Serve the Sweet and Spicy Glazed Tempeh over cooked rice or quinoa.

Enjoy your Sweet and Spicy Glazed Tempeh!

Tips:

- Adjust the level of spiciness by adding more or less sriracha sauce.
- Feel free to add extra vegetables like bell peppers, broccoli, or snap peas for added texture and flavor.
- This glazed tempeh is versatile and can be served in wraps, bowls, or as a topping for salads.

Vegan Spinach and Artichoke Dip

Ingredients:

- 1 cup raw cashews, soaked in hot water for 1-2 hours or overnight
- 1 tablespoon olive oil
- 1 medium onion, finely chopped
- 3 cloves garlic, minced
- 1 can (14 oz) artichoke hearts, drained and chopped
- 1 package (10 oz) frozen chopped spinach, thawed and excess water squeezed out
- 1/2 cup nutritional yeast
- 1/2 cup vegan mayonnaise
- 1 tablespoon lemon juice
- 1 teaspoon onion powder
- 1/2 teaspoon garlic powder
- Salt and pepper to taste
- 1/2 cup unsweetened almond milk (or any plant-based milk)

Instructions:

Prepare Cashews:
- Drain and rinse the soaked cashews.

Make Cashew Cream:
- In a blender, blend the cashews with 1/2 cup almond milk until smooth and creamy. Set aside.

Sauté Onion and Garlic:
- In a skillet, heat olive oil over medium heat. Sauté chopped onion and minced garlic until softened.

Add Spinach and Artichokes:
- Add chopped artichoke hearts and thawed, squeezed spinach to the skillet. Cook for a few minutes until any excess liquid evaporates.

Make Dip Base:
- Stir in the cashew cream, nutritional yeast, vegan mayonnaise, lemon juice, onion powder, garlic powder, salt, and pepper. Mix well to combine.

Adjust Consistency:
- Adjust the consistency by adding more almond milk if needed. The dip should be thick and creamy.

Heat Through:
- Heat the mixture through, allowing the flavors to meld. Stir frequently to prevent sticking.

Serve:
- Transfer the Vegan Spinach and Artichoke Dip to a serving dish. You can also transfer it to an oven-safe dish if you want to bake it.

Optional Baking:
- If baking, preheat the oven to 350°F (180°C) and bake for 15-20 minutes or until the top is golden and bubbly.

Garnish and Enjoy:
- Garnish with additional nutritional yeast or fresh herbs. Serve with tortilla chips, pita bread, or vegetable sticks.

Enjoy your Vegan Spinach and Artichoke Dip!

Tips:

- Adjust the seasonings to your taste. You can add more lemon juice for acidity or extra garlic for a stronger flavor.
- If you prefer a baked dip, transfer the mixture to an oven-safe dish, sprinkle with vegan cheese, and bake until bubbly and golden.

Vegan Blueberry Oat Muffins

Ingredients:

- 1 cup rolled oats
- 1 cup unsweetened almond milk (or any plant-based milk)
- 1 tablespoon apple cider vinegar
- 1 1/2 cups all-purpose flour
- 1/2 cup whole wheat flour
- 1 1/2 teaspoons baking powder
- 1/2 teaspoon baking soda
- 1/2 teaspoon salt
- 1/2 cup maple syrup or agave nectar
- 1/4 cup melted coconut oil or vegetable oil
- 1 teaspoon vanilla extract
- 1 1/2 cups fresh or frozen blueberries
- Zest of 1 lemon (optional)
- Turbinado sugar for sprinkling on top (optional)

Instructions:

Preheat Oven:
- Preheat your oven to 375°F (190°C). Line a muffin tin with paper liners or grease the cups.

Prepare Oat Mixture:
- In a bowl, combine rolled oats and almond milk. Stir in the apple cider vinegar and let it sit for about 5 minutes to create a buttermilk-like mixture.

Mix Dry Ingredients:
- In a large bowl, whisk together all-purpose flour, whole wheat flour, baking powder, baking soda, and salt.

Combine Wet Ingredients:
- To the oat mixture, add maple syrup (or agave nectar), melted coconut oil (or vegetable oil), and vanilla extract. Mix well.

Combine Wet and Dry Mixtures:
- Pour the wet ingredients into the dry ingredients and stir until just combined. Do not overmix; a few lumps are okay.

Fold in Blueberries:
- Gently fold in the blueberries and lemon zest (if using).

Fill Muffin Cups:

- Spoon the batter into the muffin cups, filling each about 2/3 full.

Optional Topping:
- If desired, sprinkle a small amount of turbinado sugar on top of each muffin for a crunchy topping.

Bake:
- Bake in the preheated oven for 18-22 minutes or until a toothpick inserted into the center comes out clean.

Cool and Enjoy:
- Allow the muffins to cool in the tin for a few minutes before transferring them to a wire rack to cool completely.

Enjoy your Vegan Blueberry Oat Muffins!

Tips:

- If using frozen blueberries, toss them in a little flour before folding into the batter to prevent them from sinking to the bottom.
- Feel free to add chopped nuts or seeds for extra texture and flavor.
- Adjust the sweetness by adding more or less maple syrup/agave according to your taste.

Mediterranean Chickpea Salad

Ingredients:

- 2 cans (15 oz each) chickpeas, drained and rinsed
- 1 cup cherry tomatoes, halved
- 1 cucumber, diced
- 1/2 red onion, finely chopped
- 1/2 cup Kalamata olives, sliced
- 1/2 cup crumbled vegan feta cheese
- 1/4 cup fresh parsley, chopped
- 1/4 cup fresh mint, chopped
- 3 tablespoons extra virgin olive oil
- 2 tablespoons red wine vinegar
- 1 clove garlic, minced
- 1 teaspoon dried oregano
- Salt and pepper to taste
- Lemon wedges for serving (optional)

Instructions:

Prepare Chickpeas:
- If using canned chickpeas, drain and rinse them thoroughly.

Make Dressing:
- In a small bowl, whisk together olive oil, red wine vinegar, minced garlic, dried oregano, salt, and pepper to create the dressing.

Combine Salad Ingredients:
- In a large salad bowl, combine chickpeas, cherry tomatoes, diced cucumber, chopped red onion, sliced Kalamata olives, vegan feta cheese, fresh parsley, and fresh mint.

Toss with Dressing:
- Pour the dressing over the salad ingredients and toss gently to coat everything evenly.

Chill:
- Allow the Mediterranean Chickpea Salad to chill in the refrigerator for at least 30 minutes to let the flavors meld.

Serve:

- Serve the salad chilled, and garnish with additional fresh herbs if desired. Optionally, provide lemon wedges for squeezing over the salad before serving.

Enjoy your Mediterranean Chickpea Salad!

Tips:

- You can customize this salad by adding ingredients like diced bell peppers, artichoke hearts, or roasted red peppers.
- Adjust the quantity of olive oil, vinegar, and seasonings according to your taste preference.
- This salad can be served as a side dish, main course, or as a filling for wraps or pitas.

Vegan Chocolate Banana Bread

Ingredients:

- 3 ripe bananas, mashed
- 1/2 cup unsweetened applesauce
- 1/4 cup melted coconut oil or vegetable oil
- 1/2 cup granulated sugar
- 1 teaspoon vanilla extract
- 1 cup all-purpose flour
- 1/2 cup cocoa powder
- 1 teaspoon baking soda
- 1/2 teaspoon baking powder
- 1/4 teaspoon salt
- 1/2 cup vegan chocolate chips (optional)
- Chopped nuts for topping (optional)

Instructions:

Preheat Oven:
- Preheat your oven to 350°F (175°C). Grease a 9x5-inch loaf pan.

Mash Bananas:
- In a large bowl, mash the ripe bananas with a fork.

Add Wet Ingredients:
- Add the applesauce, melted coconut oil, granulated sugar, and vanilla extract to the mashed bananas. Mix well.

Sift Dry Ingredients:
- In a separate bowl, sift together the all-purpose flour, cocoa powder, baking soda, baking powder, and salt.

Combine Wet and Dry Mixtures:
- Add the dry ingredients to the wet ingredients, stirring until just combined. Be careful not to overmix.

Fold in Chocolate Chips:
- If using, fold in the vegan chocolate chips.

Transfer to Loaf Pan:
- Pour the batter into the greased loaf pan, spreading it evenly.

Optional Toppings:
- Sprinkle chopped nuts on top if desired.

Bake:

- Bake in the preheated oven for 50-60 minutes or until a toothpick inserted into the center comes out clean or with a few moist crumbs.

Cool:
- Allow the Vegan Chocolate Banana Bread to cool in the pan for about 10 minutes before transferring it to a wire rack to cool completely.

Slice and Serve:
- Once cooled, slice and serve. Enjoy your Vegan Chocolate Banana Bread!

Tips:

- Adjust the level of sweetness by adding more or less sugar according to your preference.
- You can substitute other plant-based sweeteners like maple syrup or agave nectar for the granulated sugar.
- Make sure to use ripe bananas for optimal sweetness and flavor.
- Customize the recipe by adding nuts, seeds, or dried fruit to the batter.

Creamy Vegan Mac and Cheese

Ingredients:

- 12 oz (about 3 cups) elbow macaroni or any pasta of your choice
- 1 cup peeled and diced potatoes
- 1/4 cup peeled and diced carrots
- 1/3 cup raw cashews, soaked in hot water for 1-2 hours or overnight
- 1/2 cup nutritional yeast
- 1/4 cup refined coconut oil or vegan butter
- 1/2 cup unsweetened almond milk (or any plant-based milk)
- 1 tablespoon lemon juice
- 1 teaspoon white or yellow miso paste (optional, for umami flavor)
- 1/2 teaspoon garlic powder
- 1/2 teaspoon onion powder
- 1/2 teaspoon turmeric powder (for color)
- Salt and pepper to taste
- Bread crumbs for topping (optional)

Instructions:

Cook Pasta:
- Cook the pasta according to the package instructions. Drain and set aside.

Prepare Vegetables:
- In a separate pot, boil the diced potatoes and carrots until they are tender. Drain and set aside.

Make Cashew Cream:
- In a blender, blend the soaked cashews, nutritional yeast, almond milk, lemon juice, miso paste (if using), garlic powder, onion powder, turmeric powder, salt, and pepper until smooth and creamy.

Combine Ingredients:
- In a large saucepan, melt the coconut oil or vegan butter. Add the cooked potatoes, carrots, and the cashew cream mixture. Stir well to combine.

Blend Until Smooth:
- Use an immersion blender or transfer the mixture to a regular blender and blend until smooth and creamy.

Adjust Consistency:

- Adjust the consistency by adding more almond milk if needed. The sauce should be creamy and pourable.

Combine with Pasta:
- Pour the creamy vegan cheese sauce over the cooked pasta. Gently stir to coat the pasta evenly with the sauce.

Optional Toppings:
- If desired, sprinkle bread crumbs on top for a crunchy texture.

Serve:
- Serve the Creamy Vegan Mac and Cheese immediately. Enjoy!

Tips:

- You can add a pinch of cayenne pepper or smoked paprika for a hint of spice.
- Customize the recipe by adding sautéed vegetables, such as spinach, mushrooms, or cherry tomatoes.
- Adjust the thickness of the sauce by adding more or less almond milk according to your preference.

Roasted Red Pepper and Walnut Pesto Pasta

Ingredients:

For the Pesto:

- 2 large red bell peppers, roasted and peeled
- 1/2 cup walnuts, toasted
- 2 cloves garlic
- 1/2 cup nutritional yeast
- 1/2 cup fresh basil leaves
- 1/4 cup fresh parsley leaves
- 1/2 cup extra-virgin olive oil
- Salt and pepper to taste
- Juice of 1 lemon

For the Pasta:

- 12 oz (about 340g) pasta of your choice
- Salt for boiling pasta
- Additional olive oil for drizzling
- Fresh basil and parsley for garnish
- Vegan Parmesan or nutritional yeast for topping (optional)

Instructions:

1. Roast Red Peppers:

- Preheat the oven broiler. Place whole red bell peppers on a baking sheet and broil, turning occasionally until the skin is charred and blistered. Transfer peppers to a bowl, cover with a towel, and let them steam for about 10 minutes. Peel off the skin, remove seeds, and roughly chop the peppers.

2. Toast Walnuts:

- In a dry skillet over medium heat, toast the walnuts until they become fragrant, about 3-5 minutes. Be careful not to burn them.

3. Prepare Pesto:

- In a food processor, combine the roasted red peppers, toasted walnuts, garlic, nutritional yeast, basil, parsley, olive oil, salt, pepper, and lemon juice. Blend until smooth and well combined.

4. Cook Pasta:

- Cook the pasta in a large pot of salted boiling water according to the package instructions. Drain and reserve a cup of pasta water.

5. Combine Pasta and Pesto:

- In a large mixing bowl, toss the cooked pasta with the roasted red pepper and walnut pesto until evenly coated. If the pesto is too thick, add a bit of reserved pasta water to reach your desired consistency.

6. Drizzle with Olive Oil:

- Drizzle with additional olive oil and toss to combine.

7. Serve:

- Serve the Roasted Red Pepper and Walnut Pesto Pasta warm. Garnish with fresh basil, parsley, and vegan Parmesan or nutritional yeast if desired.

8. Enjoy your flavorful Roasted Red Pepper and Walnut Pesto Pasta!

Tips:

- Feel free to customize the pesto by adding ingredients like sun-dried tomatoes or a pinch of red pepper flakes for some heat.
- Adjust the thickness of the pesto by adding more olive oil or pasta water as needed.
- For extra protein, you can add cooked chickpeas or grilled tofu to the pasta.

Vegan Mango Coconut Chia Pudding

Ingredients:

- 1/4 cup chia seeds
- 1 cup coconut milk (canned or homemade)
- 1 ripe mango, peeled and diced
- 1-2 tablespoons maple syrup or agave nectar (optional, depending on your sweetness preference)
- 1/2 teaspoon vanilla extract
- Shredded coconut and additional mango slices for topping (optional)

Instructions:

Prepare Chia Seed Mixture:
- In a bowl, combine chia seeds and coconut milk. Stir well to ensure the chia seeds are evenly distributed in the liquid.

Sweeten and Flavor:
- Add maple syrup or agave nectar (if using) and vanilla extract to the chia seed mixture. Stir again to combine.

Chill:
- Cover the bowl and refrigerate the chia seed mixture for at least 4 hours or overnight. This allows the chia seeds to absorb the liquid and create a pudding-like consistency.

Blend Mango:
- In a blender or food processor, puree the diced mango until smooth.

Layer Pudding and Mango Puree:
- Once the chia pudding has set, layer it with the mango puree in serving glasses or jars.

Top with Coconut:
- Optionally, top the Vegan Mango Coconut Chia Pudding with shredded coconut and additional mango slices for added texture and flavor.

Serve Chilled:
- Serve the pudding chilled and enjoy the tropical goodness!

Optional Variations:
- Feel free to experiment with other fruit purees or toppings such as berries, kiwi, or passion fruit.

Enjoy your Vegan Mango Coconut Chia Pudding!

Tips:

- Adjust the sweetness by adding more or less maple syrup/agave according to your taste.
- Use full-fat coconut milk for a creamier pudding, or lighten it up with lite coconut milk.
- If you prefer a smoother texture, you can blend the entire chia pudding mixture after it has set.

www.ingramcontent.com/pod-product-compliance
Lightning Source LLC
LaVergne TN
LVHW081602060526
838201LV00054B/2023